# BUDGET JUSTIFICATIONS

The United States
Department of the Interior

# JUSTIFICATIONS

and Performance Information
Fiscal Year 2015

# BUREAU OF OCEAN ENERGY MANAGEMENT

NOTICE: These budget justifications are prepared for the Interior, Environment and Related Agencies Appropriations Subcommittees. Approval for release of the justifications prior to their printing in the public record of the Subcommittee hearings may be obtained through the Office of Budget of the Department of the Interior.

# BUREAU OF OCEAN ENERGY MANAGEMENT
## FY 2015 PERFORMANCE BUDGET

## Table of Contents

# Table of Figures

# Table of Tables

# Bureau of Ocean Energy Management
## Acronyms

| | |
|---|---|
| APD | Application for Permit to Drill |
| BLM | Bureau of Land Management |
| BOEM | Bureau of Ocean Energy Management |
| BOEMRE | Bureau of Ocean Energy Management, Regulation & Enforcement |
| BSEE | Bureau of Safety and Environmental Enforcement |
| CEIL | Center for Environmental Innovation and Leadership |
| CEQ | Council on Environmental Quality |
| CFO | Chief Financial Officer |
| CFR | Code of Federal Regulations |
| COP | Construction and Operation Plan |
| CR | Continuing Resolution |
| DOD | Department of Defense |
| DOCD | Development Operation Coordination Document |
| DOI | Department of the Interior |
| DPP | Development and Production Plan |
| EIS | Environmental Impact Statement |
| EP | Exploration Plan |
| EPA | Environmental Protection Agency |
| FERC | Federal Energy Regulatory Commission |
| FTE | Full Time Equivalent |
| FWS | U.S. Fish and Wildlife Service |
| FY | Fiscal Year |
| G&G | Geological and Geophysical |
| GAO | Government Accountability Office |
| GIS | Geographical Information System |
| GPRA | Government Performance and Results Act |
| GSA | General Services Agency |
| IT | Information Technology |
| MHK | Marine Hydrokinetics |
| MMP | Marine Minerals Program |
| MMS | Minerals Management Service |
| NASA | National Aeronautics and Space Administration |
| NEPA | National Environmental Policy Act |
| NMFS | National Marine Fisheries Service |
| NOAA | National Oceanic and Atmospheric Administration |
| NOP | National Ocean Policy |
| NOPP | National Oceanographic Partnership Program |

| | |
|---|---|
| NPS | National Park Service |
| NRC | National Research Council |
| NREL | National Renewable Energy Laboratory |
| OCS | Outer Continental Shelf |
| ONRR | Office of Natural Resources Revenue |
| PEIS | Programmatic Environmental Impact Statement |
| PL | Public Law |
| ROW | Right-of-Way |
| RUE | Rights-of-Use and Easement |
| SLA | Submerged Lands Act |
| TIMS | Technical Information Management System |
| U.S.C. | United States Code |
| USGS | U.S. Geological Survey |
| WCD | Worst Case Discharge |
| WEA | Wind Energy Area |

# FY 2015 PERFORMANCE BUDGET
## Bureau of Ocean Energy Management
*Director's Preface*

*"Today we are moving closer to tapping into the enormous potential offered by offshore wind to create jobs, increase our sustainability, and strengthen our nation's competitiveness in this new energy frontier. As we experience record domestic oil and gas development, we are also working to ensure that America leads the world in developing the energy of the future."*

— Sally Jewell, U.S. Secretary of the Interior
May 3, 2013

Established on October 1, 2011, the Bureau of Ocean Energy Management (BOEM), is charged with managing the Nation's offshore resources in a balanced way that promotes efficient and environmentally responsible energy and mineral development through oil and gas leasing, renewable energy development, marine mineral leasing and a commitment to rigorous, science-based environmental review and study. BOEM plays an important role in advancing President Obama's all-of-the-above approach to expanding responsible development of domestic energy resources as part of a broad effort to secure the nation's energy future, benefit the economy, and create jobs.

Over the last year, this agency has made significant progress toward achieving a number of important priorities, including:

- **The Five Year Outer Continental Shelf (OCS) Oil and Gas Leasing Program for 2012-2017.** Since the approval of the 2012-2017 OCS Oil and Gas Leasing Five Year Program in August 2012, BOEM has worked diligently to carry out its innovative, regionally-tailored approach to offshore oil and gas leasing. During calendar year 2013, BOEM held two lease sales, which combined generated more than $1.3 billion in high bids. Three lease sales are planned for calendar year 2014 and two lease sales are planned for calendar year 2015. A comprehensive table showing the lease sale schedule provided for by the Five Year Program is included in the Conventional Energy chapter of this budget justification.

- **Conducting rigorous scientific and environmental analysis to support all stages of the OCS Lands Act process – from pre-sale planning through exploration and development.** Throughout fiscal years 2014 and 2015, BOEM will complete environmental reviews in support of mission-critical activities and lease sales included in the current Five Year Program. In 2014, BOEM will begin the NEPA process for the first Arctic lease sale under this Program, to be held in 2016. In anticipation of this, the Bureau is currently working with the National Oceanic and Atmospheric Administration (NOAA) to publish an environmental review of activities in the Arctic. In addition, BOEM recently published a Programmatic Environmental Impact Statement analyzing proposed geological and geophysical activities in the Mid- and South Atlantic, the results of which may be used to inform the development of the next Five Year Program. In its applied research program,

BOEM has leveraged partnerships with academic institutions and other Federal agencies to extend its allocated research budget, and will continue to advance those partnerships and produce top-tier scientific work in the coming year.

- **Conducting efficient and thorough reviews of exploration and development plans.** Consistent with strengthened environmental analyses, BOEM is committed to ensuring that its process for reviewing and approving plans is rigorous, efficient, and transparent. BOEM works collaboratively with industry throughout the review of plans, with the goals of ensuring that operators comply with BOEM's heightened operational and environmental standards and that the review process is efficient. With funding provided in FY 2014, BOEM is initiating the development of the ePlans Portal, which will modernize and streamline the plan submission and review process when fully implemented.

- **Advancing a focused policy for the Arctic.** BOEM is advancing a region-specific set of policies for the Arctic, including a targeted leasing strategy, described in the Five Year Program and focused on balancing exploration of energy resources with consideration for the environment and native communities' cultural and subsistence needs. In overseeing recent and proposed exploration activities, BOEM upholds standards that are tailored to the unique conditions of the Arctic, including extreme weather and limited supporting infrastructure. BOEM will continue these efforts this fiscal year. The importance of focused Arctic policy is highlighted within the document "Report to the Secretary of the Interior: Review of Shell's 2012 Alaska Offshore Oil and Gas Exploration Program," which underscores the importance of rigorous planning and oversight to ensure that industry meets high standards for operating in the Arctic. The March 2013 report highlighted the need to "continue to develop and refine standards and practices that are specific to the unique and challenging conditions associated with offshore oil and gas exploration on the Alaskan OCS." BOEM and the Bureau of Safety and Environmental Enforcement are currently drafting proposed rules to revise and clarify requirements for future exploratory drilling and related operations offshore Alaska. The bureaus anticipate publishing the new proposed rulemaking in FY 2014. Additionally, BOEM is working with NOAA to complete a broad environmental impact statement for seismic and exploratory activity in the Arctic.

- **Advancing a region-specific strategy for the Atlantic.** BOEM is pursuing a strategy for the Atlantic that is focused on expediting efforts to facilitate updated resource evaluation to support future leasing decisions. During FY 2014, BOEM will undertake an initiative that enables the acquisition and management of G&G data within the Mid- and South Atlantic. This will support future decision-making regarding whether, and if so, where potential offshore oil and gas lease sales in the Mid- and South Atlantic planning areas would be appropriate.

- **Making significant progress towards renewable energy leasing and development.** To date, BOEM, in consultation with its Intergovernmental Task Forces, has identified wind energy areas on the OCS offshore Rhode Island, Massachusetts, New Jersey, Delaware, Maryland, and Virginia. BOEM expects to identify additional areas offshore North Carolina and New York during FY 2014, and to identify areas offshore South Carolina during FY 2015. Identification and subsequent analysis and review of wind energy areas enable potential lease sales within those areas to move forward. BOEM is also making progress on on-siting demonstration and technology testing projects for wind and marine hydrokinetic energy offshore both the Atlantic and Pacific coasts.

- **Managing offshore sand and gravel resources.** Using funds provided through the Hurricane Sandy Supplemental Appropriation in FY 2013, BOEM's Marine Minerals Program completed seven projects and conveyed close to 8 million cubic yards of sand and gravel to restore almost 44 miles of coastline in Virginia, North Carolina, and Florida. In FY 2014, BOEM will utilize enacted funding to continue work to execute eleven agreements to restore coastline in New Jersey, North Carolina, South Carolina, and Florida. BOEM will also fund Cooperative Agreements with Atlantic coastal states, and conduct comprehensive geophysical and geological surveys to delineate additional OCS sand resources for future coastal resiliency projects. Additionally, BOEM will continue to assist with Hurricane Sandy recovery and implement other coastal restoration projects by working with states, localities, tribal governments, and Federal partners concerning site analyses, environmental issues, and leasing of OCS sediment.

The FY 2015 budget requests $169.8 million, which includes $97.3 million in offsetting collections (approximately $94.9 million from rental receipts and nearly $2.5 million from cost recovery fees). This is an increase in budget authority of $2.9 million above the FY 2014 enacted level and a $3.4 million increase in net appropriations. The request will support critical ongoing efforts and important initiatives detailed within the General Statement of this book. The requests for funding increases are limited, reflecting difficult tradeoffs given the current tight fiscal constraints. BOEM's FY 2015 request reflects a careful analysis of the resources needed to develop the Bureau's capacity and to execute its functions carefully, responsibly, and efficiently. Consistent with the overall contours of BOEM's FY 2015 request, the targeted increase is vital to BOEM's mission and critical to advancing Administration priorities.

*This page intentionally left blank.*

# FY 2015 PERFORMANCE BUDGET
## Bureau of Ocean Energy Management
### *General Statement*

The Bureau of Ocean Energy Management (BOEM) manages the environmentally and economically responsible development of the Nation's offshore energy and mineral resources. The Bureau's functions include offshore leasing, resource and economic evaluation, review and administration of oil and gas exploration and development plans, renewable energy development, National Environmental Policy Act (NEPA) analysis, and environmental studies. BOEM's functions are described in more detail in the following narrative.

> ## *Bureau of Ocean Energy Management Mission*
>
> *The mission of the Bureau of Ocean Energy Management is to manage development of the nation's offshore energy and mineral resources in an environmentally and economically responsible way.*

**Leasing.** BOEM is responsible for conventional and renewable energy and marine mineral leasing policies and programs. For conventional energy, this applies to all Outer Continental Shelf (OCS) leasing and development issues for oil, gas and other marine minerals. This includes developing a Five Year Oil and Gas Program and designing individual oil and gas lease sales in a way that makes oil and gas resources available, protects communities and the environment, ensures fair value to the American taxpayer, and provides incentives for diligent development of leases. For renewable energy, BOEM manages offshore leasing and oversees all activities for renewable energy and alternate-use projects. BOEM also makes OCS sand and gravel resources available for coastal restoration and protection projects.

**Plan Administration.** BOEM conducts in-depth reviews of exploration plans, development and production plans, and development operation coordination documents to ensure that plan activities are conducted in accordance with applicable laws, regulations, and lease terms. BOEM is committed to ensuring that its process for reviewing and approving plans is rigorous, efficient, and transparent to industry. BOEM works collaboratively with industry throughout the review of plans, with the goals of ensuring that operators comply with rigorous operational and environmental requirements and that the review process is efficient.

**Environmental Science.** BOEM is committed to ensuring that both conventional and renewable energy decisions are informed by the best available science. BOEM facilitates top-quality research by talented scientists from a range of disciplines and targeted to support policy needs and priorities. Applied research through the studies program informs the environmental reviews that BOEM prepares to support decision-making. To ensure their full integration, BOEM oversees both applied research and environmental review processes.

**Economics.** BOEM conducts economic, statistical, engineering, and cost-benefit analyses for Bureau and Departmental energy and minerals programs. The objective is to evaluate, recommend, design, and implement policies and statutory requirements relating to lease terms, bidding systems, auction designs, rulemaking, revenue forecasts, post-sale bid adequacy determinations, and revenue sharing with the states. This work involves broad interfaces with other bureaus and offices within the Department of the Interior (DOI), with other Federal departments and offices, and with Congressional energy resource committees.

**Resource Evaluation.** BOEM's resource evaluation program includes: fair market value determination, which is focused on thoroughly assessing the oil and gas potential and associated economic value of OCS tracts offered for lease; resource assessment, which is focused on identifying geologic plays on the OCS that offer the highest potential for hydrocarbon resources; and reserves inventory, or the development of independent estimates of economically recoverable amounts of oil and gas contained within discovered fields obtained by conducting field reserve studies. Program activities also include acquisition and analysis of geological and geophysical (G&G) data, as well as permitting of G&G activity to ensure that pre-lease exploration, prospecting, and scientific research operations in Federal waters are conducted in a balanced way that protects wildlife and the environment, as well as cultural and archaeological resources, and minimizes conflicts with other uses of the OCS – such as subsistence use and exploration and development on nearby leases.

**Renewable Energy Development.** The Energy Policy Act of 2005 authorizes DOI to grant leases, easements, or rights-of-way for activities on the OCS that produce or support production, transportation, or transmission of energy from renewable sources. Renewable energy and alternate-use projects can include wind, wave and ocean current energy, as well as projects that make alternative use of existing oil and gas platforms in Federal waters. The Department and BOEM have continued to advance renewable energy efforts, as part of the President's all-of-the-above strategy. This includes advancing the Smart from the Start initiative, which aims to facilitate efficient and environmentally responsible siting, leasing, and construction of new wind energy projects in the Atlantic. BOEM is also working to facilitate renewable energy off the coast of the Pacific States.


**BUREAU BUDGET STRUCTURE**

Budget activities for BOEM are funded through the Ocean Energy Management (OEM) account and support resource evaluation, planning, and leasing of the Nation's offshore energy and mineral resources in an appropriately balanced way that promotes economic development, energy independence, and environmental protection. The OEM account is comprised of the following activities:

**Renewable Energy.** This activity funds renewable energy activities for the OCS, including program development and implementation and compliance work in support of competitive and noncompetitive leasing actions; review of site assessment and construction and operations plans; consultation with state and local governments, Federal agencies, tribes, and other stakeholders; and development of a multipurpose marine cadastre. The renewable energy activity supports the Smart from the Start initiative described above.

**Conventional Energy.** Activities funded through Conventional Energy include: OCS oil and gas leasing, and the development of the Five Year Program; surveying OCS boundaries; implementing the lease sale process; administering leases; and reviewing exploration and development plans and G&G permit applications. Resource evaluation is a critical component of the program that provides the information needed to support program decision making. This includes technical and economic analysis; tract evaluation; assessment and modeling; conservation of resources; reserves inventories; G&G data acquisition; and fair market value determinations. Also funded through Conventional Energy are marine planning and activities involving marine minerals other than oil and gas.

**Environmental Programs.** This activity funds environmental analyses such as environmental impact statements and environmental assessments needed to assess potential environmental impacts of proposed actions in accordance with NEPA and related regulations. It also supports applied research through the Environmental Studies Program, designed to support policy priorities and ensure that environmental reviews conducted in support of policy decisions incorporate rigorous scientific analysis.

**General Support Services.** This activity funds shared support services for the Bureau. These expenses relate to: administrative services including finance, human resources, procurement, facilities, information technology and management, and equal employment services; rental and security of office space; workers' compensation and unemployment compensation; voice and data communications; centrally-provided services funded by the Department's Working Capital Fund; annual building maintenance contracts; mail services; and printing costs. BOEM obtains most of these services from BSEE through a reimbursable service agreement.

**Executive Direction.** This activity funds Bureau-wide leadership, direction, management, coordination, communications strategies, outreach, and regulatory development. It includes functions such as budget, congressional and public affairs, policy analysis, and regulations. The Office of the Director is funded within this activity and is responsible for providing general policy guidance and overall leadership within BOEM. The Director's Office also oversees administrative direction and coordination for all administrative activities within BOEM.

Functions and funds within these activities are divided among program offices located at headquarters and regional offices, which are described below. BOEM's organizational structure is designed to advance each of the elements of its mission. The national functions are grouped into three offices headquartered in the Greater Washington D.C. area and focus on strategic resource development, environmental analysis and applied science, and offshore renewable energy development. Additionally, BOEM has three regional offices that handle a number of key agency responsibilities. This structure is summarized below and displayed in the organizational chart in Figure 1.

**Figure 1: BOEM Organizational Chart**

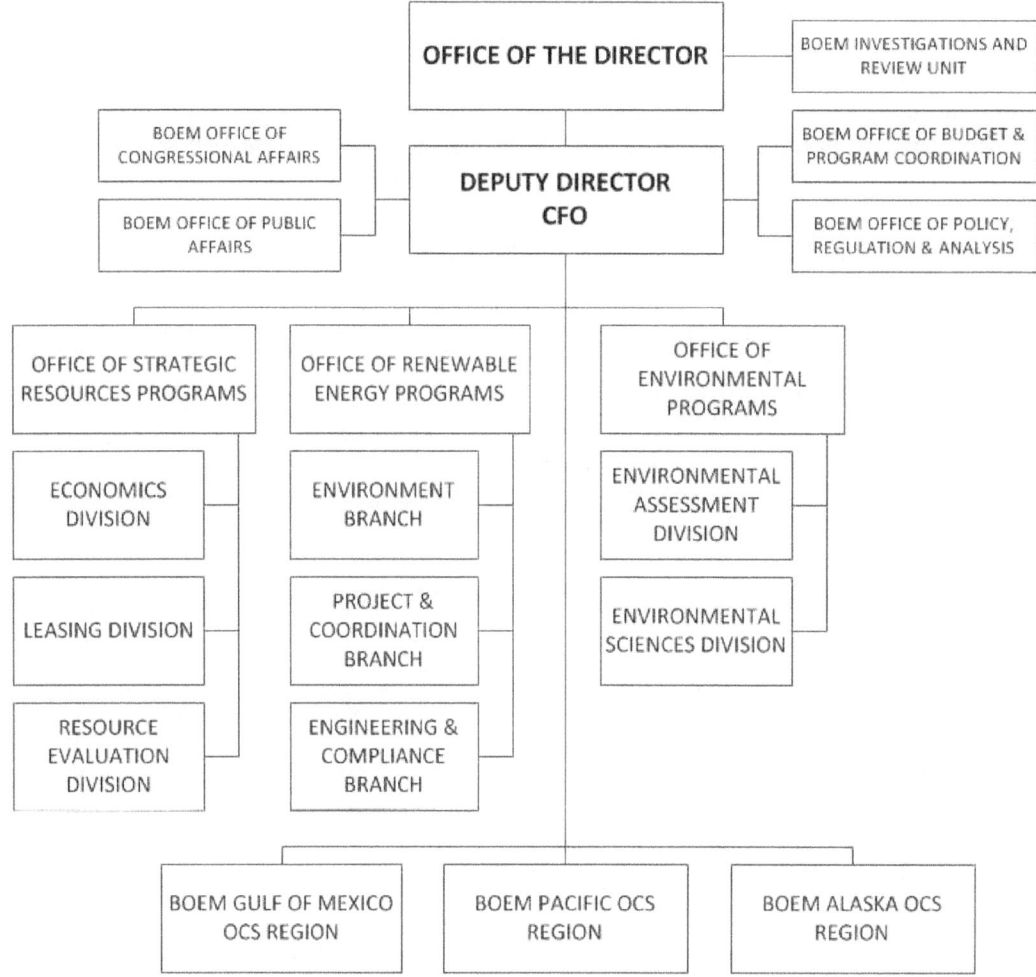

**The Office of Strategic Resources Programs** is committed to managing offshore resources to help meet the Nation's energy and resource needs by developing programs to provide access to, and fair return to the American taxpayer for offshore energy and mineral resources through strategic planning and resource and economic evaluation. This includes: development of the Five Year Program; assessment of mineral resource potential, tracking of inventories of oil and gas reserves, and development of production projections; and economic evaluation to ensure the receipt of fair value through lease sales and lease terms.

**The Office of Renewable Energy Programs** advances a sustainable OCS renewable energy future through interactive site planning and environmentally responsible operations and energy generation. Among other things, this office supports the Secretary's Smart from the Start initiative to facilitate siting, leasing, and construction of new projects, spurring the responsible development of offshore wind resources off the Atlantic coast.

**The Office of Environmental Programs** conducts and oversees applied science and environmental assessments at every stage of the offshore energy development planning process –

for both conventional and renewable energy activities – in order to inform decisions for environmentally responsible ocean energy and mineral development. BOEM also ensures that it manages, mitigates, monitors, and adapts to the potential consequences of exploring for and developing these resources. As a responsible steward, BOEM must also meet its stakeholder engagement responsibilities. To fulfill these responsibilities, BOEM's environmental programs are comprised of a diverse team of scientists, policy specialists, and technical professionals, whose expertise spans archaeology, biology, oceanography, environmental, and social disciplines.

BOEM has three regional offices – Gulf of Mexico, Pacific and Alaska – which are located in New Orleans, Louisiana; Camarillo, California; and Anchorage, Alaska, respectively. The regional offices are integrated into the national programs and are integral to all aspects of each program's responsibilities, especially oil and gas resource evaluations, environmental studies and assessments, leasing activities, review of exploration and development plans, fair market value determinations, and G&G permitting.

Headquarter and regional offices work together to implement BOEM's various activities. In addition, strong partnerships with other Federal agencies, state and local governments, environmental and other interest groups, the general public, and the oil and gas and renewable energy industries enable the regional offices to best coordinate development to fulfill BOEM's resource management responsibilities.

## FY 2015 PERFORMANCE BUDGET REQUEST

Funding for BOEM is requested through the OEM appropriation account. The OEM appropriation is partially offset by a portion of OCS rental collections and cost recovery fees.

In FY 2015, BOEM requests $169.8 million in total budget authority, an increase of $2.9 million over the FY 2014 enacted level, as shown in Table 1. BOEM's request includes offsetting collections of $94.9 million from rental receipts and $2.5 million from cost recovery fees. This results in a requested increase of $3.4 million in net direct appropriations.

## Table 1: Summary of BOEM Budget Request

*Dollars in Thousands*

| BOEM | 2013 Actual | 2014 Enacted | 2015 Budget Request | vs. 2014 Enacted |
|---|---|---|---|---|
| **Ocean Energy Management** | | | | |
| Renewable Energy | 18,537 | 23,656 | 23,104 | -552 |
| Conventional Energy | 46,115 | 49,441 | 49,633 | +192 |
| Environmental Programs | 60,578 | 63,218 | 65,712 | +2,494 |
| General Support Services | 12,149 | 14,320 | 15,002 | +682 |
| Executive Direction | 15,223 | 16,256 | 16,319 | +63 |
| **Total OEM** | **152,602** | **166,891** | **169,770** | **+2,879** |
| Rental Receipts | -94,029 | -95,162 | -94,868 | +294 |
| Cost Recovery Fees | -1,984 | -2,729 | -2,480 | +249 |
| **Total Offsetting Collections** | **-96,013** | **-97,891** | **-97,348** | **+543** |
| **TOTAL, BOEM** | **56,589** | **69,000** | **72,422** | **+3,422** |

## FY 2015 BUDGET HIGHLIGHTS

BOEM's FY 2015 Budget request includes limited funding increases, reflecting difficult tradeoffs given the current tight fiscal constraints. The BOEM FY 2015 request reflects a careful analysis of the resources needed to develop the agency's capacity and to execute its functions carefully, responsibly, and efficiently. The request includes increases for fixed costs and the programmatic environmental impact statement (EIS) for the 2017-2022 Five Year Program. The request also reflects an adjustment resulting from a revised offsetting collections estimate. Table 2 below shows the following proposed changes relative to the FY 2014 enacted level.

**Table 2: Analysis of Budgetary Changes 2014-2015**

| Activity | Program Change | Total BA | Offsetting | Net | FTE |
|---|---|---|---|---|---|
| **Bureau of Ocean Energy Management** Analysis of 2015 Budgetary Changes *Dollars in Thousands* | | | | | |
| **BOEM FY 2014 ENACTED** | | **166,891** | **-97,891** | **69,000** | **552** |
| | | | | | |
| Bureau-Wide | FY 2015 Fixed Costs | +1,462 | | | |
| Offsetting Collections | Change in Estimated Collections | | +543 | | |
| Renewable Energy | Programmatic Reduction | -617 | | | |
| Conventional Energy | Programmatic Reduction | -161 | | | |
| Environmental Programs | Programmatic EIS for Five Year Program | +2,500 | | | |
| Environmental Programs | Programmatic Reduction | -206 | | | |
| General Support Services | Programmatic Reduction | -46 | | | |
| Executive Direction | Programmatic Reduction | -53 | | | |
| **FY 2015 Budgetary Changes** | | **+2,879** | **+543** | | **+0** |
| | | | | | |
| **BOEM FY 2015 BUDGET REQUEST** | | **169,770** | **-97,348** | **72,422** | **552** |

**FY 2015 Fixed Costs (+$1,462,000; 0 FTE).** The FY 2015 Budget request fully funds fixed costs for the Bureau. A more detailed explanation of these costs can be found in the Fixed Costs table in the Bureau Budget Tables chapter.

**Change in Estimated Offsetting Collections (+$543,000; 0 FTE).** Based on the latest economic assumptions, BOEM projects its estimated offsetting collections to decrease by approximately $543,000 – from $97.9 million in FY 2014 to $97.3 million in FY 2015 – resulting in a need for increased direct appropriations to maintain an overall funding level comparable to the FY 2014 enacted level.

**Programmatic EIS for 2017-2022 Five Year Program (+$2,500,000; 0 FTE).** BOEM is requesting funds to conduct a comprehensive programmatic environmental impact statement, which is required for BOEM to begin work on the next Five Year Oil and Gas Leasing Program.

**Programmatic Reductions (-$1,083,000; 0 FTE).** In order to support BOEM's highest priority needs in FY 2015, the Bureau will modestly reduce programmatic funding across activities and realize additional savings by further implementing administrative restrictions on travel, training, and the filling of lower priority positions, similar to the measures taken during FY 2013.

**Federal Oil and Gas Reforms.** The 2015 budget includes a proposed package of legislative and administrative proposals to reform the management of Interior's onshore and offshore oil and gas programs, with a key focus on improving the return to taxpayers from the sale of these Federal resources and on improving transparency and oversight. Proposed changes fall into three general categories: advancing royalty reforms; encouraging diligent development of oil and gas leases; and improving revenue collection processes.

Royalty reforms include evaluating minimum royalty rates for oil, gas, and similar products; adjusting the onshore oil and gas royalty rate; analyzing a price-based tiered royalty rate; and repealing legislatively mandated royalty relief. Diligent development requirements include shorter primary lease terms, stricter enforcement of lease terms, and monetary incentives to get leases into production, e.g., a new per-acre fee on nonproducing leases. Revenue collection improvements include simplification of the royalty valuation process, elimination of interest accruals on company overpayments of royalties, and permanent repeal of the Department's authority to accept in-kind royalty payments. Collectively, these reforms will generate roughly $2.5 billion in net revenue to the Treasury over ten years, of which nearly $1.7 billion would result from statutory changes. Many states will also benefit from higher Federal revenue sharing payments as a result of these reforms.

## SECRETARIAL INITIATIVES

**Powering Our Future and Responsible Use of Our Resources.** Through early planning, thoughtful mitigation, and the application of sound science, Interior is working to ensure the Administration's all-of-the-above energy strategy includes not only traditional sources, but also the further development of new, cleaner resources to help mitigate the causes of climate change. The President's budget for BOEM proposes $169.8 million, an increase of $2.9 million for energy related activities in support of these objectives. BOEM is constantly and diligently seeking ways to improve efficiency through the use of technology, shared services, and best practices.

In FY 2014, BOEM will begin the first phase of development for its ePlans initiative, which will reduce review processing time by 30-40 percent for exploration and development plans. This phase will enable the electronic submission of exploration and development plans by industry to BOEM. In FY 2015, BOEM will initiate the second phase of ePlans, the development of automated processes to evaluate initial industry submissions. BOEM plans to use the lessons learned from the implementation of ePlans phase one for the development of its FY 2015 efforts to add functionality that will facilitate the issuance of G&G permits.

In addition to streamlining its review of plans, BOEM will also initiate a programmatic environmental impact statement in preparation for the development of the next Five Year Program. A thorough and completed five year programmatic environmental impact statement is required in order to move forward with the 2017-2022 Five Year Oil and Gas Leasing Program, which is foundational to fulfilling the requirements of the OCS Lands Act and the important missions of BOEM. The environmental impact statement will provide a concise assessment that addresses key issues throughout program implementation and provides information pertaining to environmental issues and Program alternatives. Additionally, the environmental work provides insight and consideration regarding frontier areas in the Five Year Program. By conducting and completing the programmatic environmental impact statement, BOEM will be able to move forward with the next Five Year Program and support the Administration's all-of-the-above energy strategy.

## COLLABORATIVE CONSERVATION

The FY 2015 Budget builds on the work done over the last four years on landscape-level and ecosystem-wide conservation, oceans policy, and climate adaptation, and moves toward institutionalizing the approaches and principles that the Administration has followed over the past four years with respect to conservation strategies. Conservation, as applied to environmentally responsible offshore ocean energy development, is a key component of BOEM activities. In keeping with the BOEM mission consideration of environmental impacts from oil and gas development, marine mineral activities, and renewable energy projects are taken into account prior to exploring and extracting resources. Marine planning is one such important tool used to implement ecosystem-based management, and to identify and minimize resource impacts as well as develop avoidance strategies.

The FY 2015 BOEM budget continues to support these practices through important partnerships and collaborative efforts. BOEM leverages its funds and expertise with other Federal agencies, state and local governments, academia, and industry. By contributing personnel, equipment, facilities and funds, the partners are able to extend the scope of the research to enable all partners involved to obtain maximum results from research efforts. Additionally, students may have the opportunity to learn through the collaborative projects and often their participation leads to publications in peer reviewed literature, or a Master's thesis or Doctoral dissertation.

One such example of BOEM's collaborative conservation activities with other entities is work conducted under the auspices of the National Oceanographic Partnership Program (NOPP). The NOPP is a collaborative community of Federal agencies that partners with state and local governments, academia, and industry with the goal of increasing knowledge and understanding of the ocean environment through research, including the areas of resource management, research and exploration, technology development, and ocean education. An independent peer review process is utilized to evaluate and recommend proposals submitted for the research projects solicited by NOPP members each year. NOPP encourages research that offers a component that benefits public education. Additionally, NOPP supports educational projects that directly and/or indirectly involve educators and students, and sponsors the National Ocean Sciences Bowl – a high school level national academic competition related to the study of oceans.

## ADMINISTRATION'S MANAGEMENT AGENDA

The Department of the Interior supports the President's Management Agenda to cut waste and implement a government that is more responsive and open. The BOEM budget supports the Department's plan to build upon the Accountable Government Initiative through a set of integrated enterprise reforms designed to support collaborative, evidence-based resource management decisions; efficient Information Technology (IT) Transformation; optimized programs, business processes, and facilities; and a network of innovative cost controlling measures that leverage strategic workforce alignment to realize an effective 21st Century Interior organization.

**Information Technology Transformation.** The FY 2015 request includes $74,000 for BOEM participation in the Department's IT Transformation efforts through the Department's Working Capital Fund. These funds will support IT Transformation project-level planning and coordination and the implementation of enterprise IT services.

## PERFORMANCE MANAGEMENT

The FY 2015 request provides the resources needed to carry out the mission of the Bureau of Ocean Energy Management, including renewable, conventional and environmental activities. Additionally, the Renewable Energy Program directly supports the Secretary's Priority Goal for Renewable Energy.

The FY 2014-2018 DOI Strategic Plan, in compliance with the principles of the Government Performance and Results (GPRA) Modernization Act of 2010, provides a collection of mission objectives, goals, strategies and corresponding metrics that provide an integrated and focused approach for tracking performance across a wide range of DOI programs. While the DOI Strategic Plan for FY 2014-2018 is the foundational structure for the description of program performance measurement and planning for the FY 2015 President's budget, further details for achieving the Strategic Plan's goals are presented in the DOI Annual Performance Plan and Report. Bureau and program specific plans for FY 2015 are fully consistent with the goals, outcomes, and measures described in the FY 2014-2018 version of the DOI Strategic Plan and related implementation information in the Annual Performance Plan and Report.

Within the DOI Strategic Plan for FY 2014–2018, BOEM is aligned under the Mission Area Three: *Powering Our Future and Responsible Use of the Nation's Resources.* The conventional energy and renewable energy activities are both focus areas within the DOI Strategic Plan, and environmental studies, assessments, and other activities conducted by BOEM support both of these strategies. BOEM tracks and reports a total of three GPRA measures, and associated supporting performance measures, to the Department under the three separate strategies noted below.

The conventional energy activities support Goal One: *Secure American's Energy Resources* and Strategy Three: *Manage Conventional Energy Development.* The specific GPRA measure, *Number of offshore lease sales held consistent with the Secretary's Five Year Program*, tracks the quantity of lease sales conducted during the current Five Year Program. The previously mentioned conventional energy GPRA measures and their supporting performance measures, which are reported within the DOI's Annual Performance Plan and Report, are noted in the following table.

**Table 3: Performance: Manage Conventional Energy Development**

| Mission Area 3: Powering Our Future and Responsible Use of the Nation's Resources<br>Goal #1: Secure America's Energy Resources<br>Strategy #3: Manage Conventional Energy Development |
| :---: |

| Outputs, Supporting Performance Measures, and/or Milestones | 2010 Actual | 2011 Actual | 2012 Actual | 2013 Plan | 2013 Actual | 2014 Plan | 2015 Plan |
| --- | --- | --- | --- | --- | --- | --- | --- |
| **GPRA Measure:** Number of offshore lease sales held consistent with the Secretary's Five-Year Oil and Gas Program | 1 | - | 2 | 3 | 3 | 3 | 2 |
| Number of blocks/tracts evaluated | 8,233 | 24,870 | 14,612 | 9,300 | 12,200 | 9,300 | 11,000 |
| Maintain the ratio of 1.8 to 1 (+/-0.4) of accepted high bids to BOEM's estimated value [1] | 1.8 to 1 | N/A | 2.013 to 1 | 1.8 to 1 (+/- 0.4) | 2.116 to 1 (+/- 0.4) | 1.8 to 1 (+/- 0.4) | 1.8 to 1 (+/- 0.4) |
| Percent of Environmental Studies Program (ESP) projects rated "Moderately Effective" or better by BOEM internal customers | 91% (10/11) | 91% (21/23) | 95% (21/22) | 88% (N/A) | 96% (22/23) | 88% (N/A) | 88% (N/A) |

[1] This measure compares the accepted high bid on each tract to the government's estimated value for that tract. Industry corporate strategy with respect to acquiring specific acreage could lead to a company raising its bid above this analytical value to improve their chances of winning the lease. BOEM estimates are based on a discounted cash flow analysis of a tract and are not designed to predict the high bid. Therefore, the value of this indicator should always be greater than one to achieve fair value for OCS leases. The annual target ratio of 1.8 to 1 means that on average, the industry bids received are expected to be $1.80 (+/-0.4) for every dollar of the estimated value for each tract.

Additionally, the conventional energy activities also support Goal Two: *Sustainably Manage Timber, Forage, and Non-energy Minerals*, Strategy Three: *Manage Non-energy Mineral Development*. The specific GPRA measure, *Number of sand and gravel requests processed for coastal restoration projects*, tracks non-energy minerals development on Departmental lands and waters, such as gold, zinc, lead, copper, iron, salt, sand, potassium, phosphate, stone, gravel, and clay, which support a broad array of uses, including medical applications, computer production, coastal restoration, automobile production, and highway construction and maintenance. This is a newly established GPRA measure and baseline results will be collected during FY 2015.

**Table 4: Performance: Manage Non-energy Mineral Development**

| Mission Area 3: Powering Our Future and Responsible Use of the Nation's Resources<br>Goal #2: Sustainably Manage Timber, Forage, and Non-energy Minerals<br>Strategy #3: Manage Non-energy Mineral Development |
| --- |

| Outputs, Supporting Performance Measures, and/or Milestones | 2010 Actual | 2011 Actual | 2012 Actual | 2013 Plan | 2013 Actual | 2014 Plan | 2015 Plan |
| --- | --- | --- | --- | --- | --- | --- | --- |
| **GPRA Measure:** Number of sand and gravel requests processed for coastal restoration projects | N/A | N/A | N/A | N/A | N/A | N/A | 10 requests annually |

The renewable energy functions support Goal One, Strategy Two: *Develop Renewable Energy Potential.* The specific GPRA measure, *Number of megawatts of approved capacity authorized on public land and the OCS for renewable energy development while ensuring full environmental review,* is a cumulative measure that tracks the cumulative number of approved megawatts based on the total capacity of the equipment to be installed, as specified in an approved construction and operations plan. The renewable energy GPRA measure and its supporting performance measures, which are reported within the DOI's Annual Performance Plan and Report, are noted in the following table.

## Table 5: Performance: Develop Renewable Energy Potential

> **Mission Area 3: Powering Our Future and Responsible Use of the Nation's Resources**
> **Goal #1: Secure America's Energy Resources**
> **Strategy #2: Develop Renewable Energy Potential**

| Outputs, Supporting Performance Measures, and/or Milestones | 2010 Actual | 2011 Actual | 2012 Actual | 2013 Plan | 2013 Actual | 2014 Plan | 2015 Plan |
|---|---|---|---|---|---|---|---|
| **GPRA Measure:** Number of megawatts of approved capacity authorized on public land and the OCS for renewable energy development while ensuring full environmental review (cumulative)[1] | N/A | N/A | 468 (cum) | 468 (cum) | 468 (cum) | 468 (cum) | 468 (cum) |
| Number of offshore renewable energy leasing or ROW/RUE grant processes initiated (i.e., first public notice issued) | 1 | 4 | 4 | 2 | 5 | 2 | 3 |
| Number of limited leases issued for offshore renewable energy testing and data collection, including §238 research leases | 4 | 0 | 0 | 2 | 0 | 3 | 1 |
| Number of commercial leases issued for offshore renewable energy generation | 0 | 1 | 0 | 4 | 2 | 3 | 6 |
| Number of right-of-way/right-of-use and easement grants issued for offshore renewable energy transmission | 0 | 0 | 0 | 0 | 0 | 1 | 0 |
| Number of offshore NEPA documents (EIS/EAs) finalized for Renewable Energy | 1 | 1 | 1 | 5 | 2 | 5 | 5 |

[1] This measure is tracked as a part of the Department of Interior Renewable Energy Priority Goal. The actuals and planned targets displayed within the table reflect BOEM's contribution toward the Department-wide Priority Goal.

## AGENCY PRIORITY GOAL: RENEWABLE ENERGY

BOEM supports the Renewable Energy Priority Goal: *Increase the approved capacity for production of energy from domestic renewable resources to support a growing economy and protect our national interests while reducing our dependence on foreign oil and climate-changing greenhouse gas emissions. By September 30, 2015, increase approved capacity authorized for renewable (solar, wind, and geothermal) energy resources affecting Department of the Interior managed lands, while ensuring full environmental review, to at least 16,500 megawatts since 2009.*

**Bureau Contribution.** BOEM supports the Renewable Energy Priority Goal primarily through its Office of Renewable Energy Programs, which advances a sustainable OCS renewable energy future through interactive site planning and environmentally responsible operations and energy generation. Support of the Secretary's Smart from the Start initiative to facilitate siting, commercial and limited leasing, and construction of new projects will spur the responsible development of offshore wind resources, consistent with this Priority Goal. Currently, the Cape Wind energy project off the coast of Massachusetts is the only permitted OCS renewable energy project contributing to this Priority Goal.

BOEM management closely monitors the renewable energy program. One of the mechanisms used to monitor the renewable energy initiative and BOEM's contribution toward the renewable energy Priority Goal is through performance metrics. The Department employs a set of internal measures and milestones to monitor and track achievement of the Priority Goal. Progress is reported and reviewed throughout the year by the Department to identify and address any need for enhanced coordination or policy measures to address barriers to the achievement of the Priority Goal. Funding for the BOEM renewable energy activities includes funding from the Renewable Energy activity as well as renewable energy studies and assessments funded through the Environmental Programs activity. BOEM's performance measures and metrics, and further information are contained within DOI's Annual Performance Plan and Report.

**Implementation Strategy.** As required by the Energy Policy Act of 2005, BOEM issues renewable energy leases and grants on a competitive basis unless it determines that no competitive interest exists. Leases and grants are generally issued through a competitive sale, but if it is determined that no competitive interest exists, then BOEM may proceed with the non-competitive lease or grant negotiation process. In either case, the developer must submit and receive approval of appropriate plans or Federal Energy Regulatory Commission license applications prior to moving forward with their proposed activities. At the end of the lease or grant term, the developer must decommission facilities in compliance with BOEM regulations.

To issue leases, BOEM must conduct a multi-step process entailing information gathering, consultation with interested and affected parties, NEPA review and compliance, and analysis in light of other applicable Federal requirements for each affected state. BOEM finalized one offshore NEPA document (either an environmental impact statement or an environmental assessment) for Renewable Energy during FY 2012 and two during FY 2013. BOEM anticipates finalizing five NEPA documents during FY 2014 and five during FY 2015. BOEM also tracks the number of offshore renewable energy leasing or right-of-way/right-of-use grant processes initiated (i.e., first public notice issued). BOEM initiated four offshore renewable energy leasing or right-of-way/right-of-use grant processes during FY 2012 and five during FY 2013. BOEM anticipates initiating two offshore renewable energy leasing or right-of-way/right-of-use grant processes during FY 2014 and three during FY 2015.

**Commercial Leases.** A commercial lease is a lease with terms and conditions which allow a person to conduct commercial activities. BOEM continues to make strides on renewable energy leasing activities. In November 2010, Secretary Salazar signed the nation's first commercial lease for wind energy development on the OCS for the Cape Wind energy project. In April 2011, the Cape Wind Energy Project construction and operations plan was approved and announced by the Secretary with an approved capacity of 468 megawatts. The Bureau reported the approval of the construction and operations plan toward the Renewable Energy Priority Goal metric, which focuses on the number of megawatts of approved capacity for renewable energy development and tracks the cumulative number of approved megawatts based on the total capacity of the equipment to be installed, as specified in an approved construction and operations plan.

BOEM issued two commercial leases in FY 2013 and anticipates being able to issue additional commercial leases for the offshore development of renewable energy in the near future after the required public consultation and environmental analyses are completed: three commercial leases during FY 2014, and six commercial leases during FY 2015.

**Limited Leases.** A limited lease is a lease with terms and conditions which allow the lessee to conduct activities on the OCS that support the production of energy but without actually producing energy for sale, distribution, or other commercial use. The number of leases issued is highly dependent upon the amount of interest and demand for the leases, and this uncertainty can lead to variability in the issuance of leases from year to year. To date, BOEM has issued four limited leases. BOEM did not issue any limited leases during FY 2012 or FY 2013, but it anticipates issuing three limited leases during FY 2014 and one limited lease during FY 2015.

**Federal/State Task Forces.** BOEM recognizes the importance of coordinating and consulting with state, local, Tribal, and Federal stakeholders to develop a comprehensive renewable energy program for the OCS. BOEM established intergovernmental task forces in states where the Governor contacted BOEM to express interest in development of offshore renewable energy. Each task force collects and shares information for all stakeholders, including BOEM, for use in its decision-making process. Task forces have been extremely productive and have helped identify areas of significant promise and interest for offshore development, in addition to providing early identification and steps toward resolution of potential conflicts. As funding permits, BOEM will continue to respond to State interest in task forces along the East Coast as well as the West Coast. During FY 2013, BOEM supported 12 Federal/state task forces for renewable energy development (Maine, Massachusetts, Rhode Island, New York, New Jersey, Delaware, Maryland, Virginia, North Carolina, South Carolina, Oregon, and Hawaii). These task forces consist of representatives of Federal agencies and state, local, and Tribal governments to facilitate coordination throughout the OCS renewable energy leasing and development process. In FY 2014 and FY 2015, BOEM will continue to support these existing state task forces and plans to establish a new task force (Florida) and support new stakeholder collaboration each year.

**Performance Metrics.** BOEM tracks and monitors performance metrics and milestones in support of the Renewable Energy Priority Goal, the results and targets for which are described above.


## AGENCY PRIORITY GOAL: CLIMATE CHANGE ADAPTATION

BOEM supports the Climate Change Adaptation Priority Goal: *By September 30, 2015, the Department of the Interior will demonstrate "maturing" implementation of climate change adaptation, as scored when implementing strategies provided in its Strategic Sustainability Performance Plan.*

**Bureau Contribution.** BOEM supports the Climate Change Adaptation Priority Goal primarily through its marine mineral and environmental activities. BOEM's most significant opportunities to catalyze resilience to climate change include the following: identifying additional sand resources to provide protection against future storms, conducting research to better understand the physical and environmental characteristics of sand bodies so resource management can be enhanced and resources are conserved, and continuing to work with our Federal, state, and local government partners to facilitate the flow of information and data for the betterment of our coastal communities.

**Implementation Strategy.** BOEM supports climate change resiliency through multiple activities. BOEM identifies and assesses climate change related impacts on and risks to BOEM's ability to accomplish its missions, operations and programs. BOEM recognizes that ongoing sea level rise and the potential for increased storm frequency and/or intensity resulting from climate change, will translate into increased coastal erosion and the need for additional sand resources to combat or recover from coastal erosion. Therefore, BOEM is actively engaged in delineating additional resources, leading a pilot effort to consider regional leases with states (thereby streamlining the leasing process), and conducting environmental studies to support effective protection of sensitive resources. BOEM is also focusing on enhanced resource management by analyzing data, conducting studies, and using tools such as Geographic Information Systems to manage risks associated with climate change, which could include sand resource depletion from increased coastal restoration projects. BOEM supports climate-resilient investments by states, tribes, and local communities through technical assistance and cooperative agreements. BOEM also contributes to coordinated interagency efforts to support climate preparedness and resilience at all levels of government, including collaborative work across agencies' regional offices and hubs, and through coordination of information, data, and tools. BOEM also provides information for the Multi-Purpose Marine Cadastre, which is a collaborative effort among a number of Federal agencies, regional planning bodies, state entities, and non-governmental organizations. Additionally, BOEM factors climate change risks in nearly all of its environmental impact statements and also partners with other agencies to leverage resources in this area. Examples of BOEM's recent partnering to further environmental efforts related to climate change include: involvement in the Interagency Arctic Research and Policy Committee; contributing to the National Climate Assessment and the latest Intergovernmental Panel on Climate Change report; engagement in the National Ocean Policy priorities surrounding climate change resiliency and adaptation; and partnering with the National

Science Foundation and French agencies to co-fund the Arctic Science Education and Engineering for Sustainability program.

**Performance Metrics.** The DOI Climate Change Working group is responsible for the Climate Change Adaptation priority goal, and reports directly to the Department of the Interior's Office of Policy Analysis.

## AGENCY PRIORITY GOAL: YOUTH STEWARDSHIP OF NATURAL AND CULTURAL RESOURCES

BOEM supports the Youth Stewardship of Natural and Cultural Resources Priority Goal: *By September 30, 2015, the Department of the Interior will provide 40,000 work and training opportunities over two fiscal years (FY 2014 and FY 2015) for individuals age 15 to 25 to support the mission of the Department.*

**Bureau Contribution.** BOEM actively supports the Youth Stewardship of Natural and Cultural Resources Priority Goal through the activities mentioned below.

**Implementation Strategy.** BOEM is actively engaged in youth initiatives and participates in the DOI Youth Task Force, Youth Alliance, and interagency working group for the development of the 21st Century Conservation Corps. Furthermore, the hiring of young people is integral to BOEM's efforts to identify and recruit high-performing candidates for our future workforce, and it has the added benefit of encouraging youth to pursue science-based studies. BOEM is also actively engaged in a number of recruitment and outreach activities that target younger generations.

**Performance Metrics.** The Department of the Interior tracks BOEM's youth employment directly through the Federal Personnel Payroll System. BOEM youth employment data is collected by the department every quarter.

*This page intentionally left blank.*

# Bureau of Ocean Energy Management
Bureau Budget Tables

## Table 6 : Budget at a Glance

### Bureau of Ocean Energy Management
### Budget at a Glance

*(dollars in thousands)*

| Account/Activity | 2013 Actual | 2014 Enacted | Changes 2014-2015 | 2015 President's Budget |
|---|---|---|---|---|
| **Ocean Energy Management** | | | | |
| Renewable Energy | 18,537 | 23,656 | -552 | 23,104 |
| *Fixed Costs* | | | *+65* | |
| *Programmatic Reduction* | | | *-617* | |
| Conventional Energy | 46,115 | 49,441 | +192 | 49,633 |
| *Fixed Costs* | | | *+353* | |
| *Programmatic Reduction* | | | *-161* | |
| Environmental Programs | 60,578 | 63,218 | +2,494 | 65,712 |
| *Fixed Costs* | | | *+200* | |
| *Programmatic EIS (2017-2022 Five Year Program)* | | | *+2,500* | |
| *Programmatic Reduction* | | | *-206* | |
| General Support Services | 12,149 | 14,320 | +682 | 15,002 |
| *Fixed Costs* | | | *+728* | |
| *Programmatic Reduction* | | | *-46* | |
| Executive Direction | 15,223 | 16,256 | +63 | 16,319 |
| *Fixed Costs* | | | *+116* | |
| *Programmatic Reduction* | | | *-53* | |
| **Total, OEM** | **152,602** | **166,891** | **+2,879** | **169,770** |
| Rental Receipts | -94,029 | -95,162 | +294 | -94,868 |
| Cost Recovery Fees | -1,984 | -2,729 | +249 | -2,480 |
| **Total, Offsetting Collections** | **-96,013** | **-97,891** | **+543** | **-97,348** |
| **NET TOTAL, BOEM** | **56,589** | **69,000** | **+3,422** | **72,422** |
| Full Time Equivalents (FTE) | 543 | 552 | - | 552 |

## Table 7 : Summary of Requirements Table

**Bureau of Ocean Energy Management**
**Summary of Requirements**
*(Dollars in Thousands)*

| | 2013 Actual | | 2014 Enacted | | Fixed Costs & Related | Program Changes (+/-) | | 2015 Request | | Changes from 2014 | |
|---|---|---|---|---|---|---|---|---|---|---|---|
| | FTE | Amount | FTE | Amount | Amount | FTE | Amount | FTE | Amount | FTE | Amount |
| **Ocean Energy Management** | | | | | | | | | | | |
| **Renewable Energy** | 47 | 18,537 | 47 | 23,656 | +65 | – | -617 | 47 | 23,104 | – | -552 |
| Direct Appropriation | | 8,194 | | 10,799 | | | | | 10,799 | | |
| Offsetting Collections | | 10,343 | | 12,857 | | | | | 12,305 | | |
| **Conventional Energy** | 261 | 46,115 | 268 | 49,441 | +353 | – | -161 | 268 | 49,633 | – | +192 |
| Direct Appropriation | | 23,108 | | 26,680 | | | | | 26,872 | | |
| Offsetting Collections | | 23,007 | | 22,761 | | | | | 22,761 | | |
| **Environmental Programs** | 148 | 60,578 | 150 | 63,218 | +200 | – | +2,294 | 150 | 65,712 | – | +2,494 |
| Direct Appropriation | | 13,091 | | 14,353 | | | | | 16,838 | | |
| Offsetting Collections | | 47,487 | | 48,865 | | | | | 48,874 | | |
| **General Support Services** | 0 | 12,149 | 0 | 14,320 | +728 | – | -46 | 0 | 15,002 | – | +682 |
| Direct Appropriation | | 3,149 | | 4,642 | | | | | 5,324 | | |
| Offsetting Collections | | 9,000 | | 9,678 | | | | | 9,678 | | |
| **Executive Direction** | 87 | 15,223 | 87 | 16,256 | +116 | – | -53 | 87 | 16,319 | – | +63 |
| Direct Appropriation | | 9,047 | | 12,526 | | | | | 12,589 | | |
| Offsetting Collections | | 6,176 | | 3,730 | | | | | 3,730 | | |
| **Total Budget Authority, BOEM** | 543 | 152,602 | 552 | 166,891 | +1,462 | | +1,417 | 552 | 169,770 | | +2,879 |
| **Offsetting Collections** | | -96,013 | | -97,891 | | | +543 | | -97,348 | | +543 |
| Rental Receipts | | -94,029 | | -95,162 | | | +294 | | -94,868 | | +294 |
| Cost Recovery Fees | | -1,984 | | -2,729 | | | +249 | | -2,480 | | +249 |
| **Net Appropriation, BOEM** | 543 | 56,589 | 552 | 69,000 | +1,462 | | +1,960 | 552 | 72,422 | | +3,422 |

## Table 8: Program and Financing Tables

| **Program and Financing** | | | |
|---|---|---|---|
| *(dollars in millions)* | | | |
| **Treasury Account ID: 14-1917** | **FY 2013** | **FY 2014** | **FY 2015** |
| **Obligations by program activity - Direct program** | | | |
| 0003 Appropriations | 61 | 72 | 72 |
| 0004 Offsetting collections | 92 | 99 | 99 |
| **0192 Total direct program** | **153** | **171** | **171** |
| **Obligations by program activity - Reimbursable program** | | | |
| 0802 Reimbursable support agreements | 6 | 6 | 6 |
| **0899 Total reimbursable program** | **6** | **6** | **6** |
| **0900 Total new obligations (direct & reimbursable)** | **159** | **177** | **177** |
| **Budgetary resources - Unobligated balance** | | | |
| 1000 Unobligated balance brought forward, Oct 1[1/] | 29 | 28 | 21 |
| 1010 Unobligated balance transferred to other accts (14-1700)[1/] | -2 | - | - |
| 1021 Recoveries of prior year unpaid obligations | 5 | 3 | 3 |
| **1050 Total unobligated balance** | **32** | **31** | **24** |
| **Budgetary resources - Budget authority** | | | |
| 1100 Appropriations, discretionary | 60 | 69 | 72 |
| 1130 Appropriations permanently reduced | -3 | - | - |
| **1160 Appropriations, discretionary (total)** | **57** | **69** | **72** |
| 1700 Collected - Offsetting collections | 167 | 98 | 97 |
| 1710 Offsetting collections transferred to other accounts (14-1700)[2/] | -64 | - | - |
| 1723 New and/or unobligated balance of spending authority from offsetting collections temporarily reduced | -5 | - | - |
| **1750 Offsetting collections, discretionary (total)** | **98** | **98** | **97** |
| **1900 Total budget authority** | **155** | **167** | **169** |
| 1930 Total budgetary resources available | 187 | 198 | 193 |
| 1941 Unexpired unobligated balance, end of year | 28 | 21 | 16 |

## Program and Financing (continued)
*(dollars in millions)*

| Treasury Account ID: 14-1917 | | FY 2013 | FY 2014 | FY 2015 |
|---|---|---|---|---|
| **Change in obligated balance - Unpaid obligations** | | | | |
| 3000 | Unpaid obligations, brought forward Oct. 1 | 107 | 106 | 84 |
| 3010 | Obligations incurred, unexpired accounts | 159 | 177 | 177 |
| 3020 | Outlays (gross) | -155 | -196 | -168 |
| 3040 | Recoveries of prior year unpaid obligations, unexpired | -5 | -3 | -3 |
| **3050** | **Unpaid obligations, end of year** | **106** | **84** | **90** |
| | | | | |
| **Change in obligated balance - Uncollected payments** | | | | |
| 3060 | Uncollected pymts, Fed sources, brought forward Oct.1 | -3 | -3 | -3 |
| **3090** | **Uncollected pymts, Fed. sources, end of year** | **-3** | **-3** | **-3** |
| | | | | |
| 3100 | Obligated balance, start of year | 104 | 103 | 81 |
| **3200** | **Obligated balance, end of year** | **103** | **81** | **87** |
| | | | | |
| **Budget authority and outlays, net** | | | | |
| **4000** | **Budget authority, gross** | **155** | **167** | **169** |
| | | | | |
| 4010 | Outlays from new discretionary authority | 78 | 113 | 114 |
| 4011 | Outlays from discretionary balances | 77 | 83 | 54 |
| **4020** | **Outlays, gross (total)** | **155** | **196** | **168** |
| | | | | |
| 4030 | Offsetting collections from Federal sources | -2 | - | - |
| 4033 | Offsetting collections from non-Federal sources | | | |
| | (Rental receipts, cost recovery fees, royalty-in-kind) | -165 | -98 | -97 |
| **4040** | **Total offsets against gross budget authority and outlays** | **-167** | **-98** | **-97** |
| | | | | |
| **4180** | **Total budget authority, net discretionary** | **-12** | **69** | **72** |
| **4190** | **Total outlays, net discretionary** | **-12** | **98** | **71** |
| | | | | |
| **Unavailable Balance: Offsetting Collections** | | | | |
| 5090 | Unavailable balance, start of year | | 5 | 5 |
| 5091 | Unavailable balance, end of year | 5 | 5 | 5 |

[1] An unobligated balance of $108 million was brought forward from BOEMRE. In accordance with the reorganization of the former Minerals Management Service, funds were transferred to BSEE (account 14-1700) and ONRR (account 14-0102). FY 2012 was first year of independent BOEM operations.

[2] Appropriations language in 2012 and 2013 required BOEM to collect BSEE's inspection fees and then transfer them from BOEM to BSEE. Public Law 113-76 amended this language beginning in 2014 so that the fees will be collected in BSEE's Offshore Safety and Environmental Enforcement account.

## Table 9: Budget Object Classification Table

### Object Classification (MAX Schedule O)
*(dollars in millions)*

| Treasury Account ID: 14-1917 | | FY 2013 | FY 2014 | FY 2015 |
|---|---|---|---|---|
| **Direct Obligations** | | | | |
| 11.1 | Personnel Compensation: Full-time permanent | 52 | 56 | 56 |
| 12.1 | Civilian personnel benefits | 16 | 17 | 17 |
| 21.0 | Travel and transportation of persons | 1 | 2 | 2 |
| 24.0 | Printing and reproduction | - | 1 | 1 |
| 25.2 | Other services from non-Federal sources | 74 | 84 | 84 |
| 26.0 | Supplies and materials | - | 1 | 1 |
| 31.0 | Equipment | 2 | 2 | 2 |
| 41.0 | Grants, subsidies, and contributions | 8 | 8 | 8 |
| **99.0** | **Total, Direct Obligations** | **153** | **171** | **171** |
| **Reimbursable Obligations** | | | | |
| 25.2 | Other services from non-Federal sources | 6 | 6 | 6 |
| **99.0** | **Total, Reimbursable Obligations** | **6** | **6** | **6** |
| **99.9** | **Total New Obligations** | **159** | **177** | **177** |

**Table 10: Justification of Fixed Costs**

## Bureau of Ocean Energy Management
Justification of Fixed Costs
*(Dollars In Thousands)*

| Fixed Cost Changes and Projections | 2015 Change |
|---|---|
| Change in Number of Paid Days | - |
| Amounts here reflect changes in pay associated with the change in the number of paid days between the 2014 and 2015. In years where there is no change in paid days, the salary impact will be zero. | |
| Pay Raise | +693 |
| The 2015 Change column reflects the change in personnel costs resulting from the 1.0% pay increase proposed in FY 2015. | |
| Employer Share of Federal Health Benefit Plans | +41 |
| The change reflects expected increases in employer's share of Federal Health Benefit Plans. | |
| Employer Share of FERS Contributions | - |
| The change reflects expected increases in employer's share of contributions to the Federal Employee Retirement System per OMB Circular A-11 guidance. | |
| Departmental Working Capital Fund | +619 |
| The change reflects expected increases in the charges for centrally billed Department services and other services through the Working Capital Fund. This includes an assessment for the Department's IT Transformation initiative. These charges are displayed in the Budget Justification for Department Management. | |
| Worker's Compensation Payments | -187 |
| The adjustment is for changes in the costs of compensating injured employees and dependents of employees who suffer accidental deaths while on duty. Costs for 2014 will reimburse the Department of Labor, Federal Employees Compensation Fund, pursuant to 5 U.S.C. 8147(b) as amended by Public Law 94-273. | |
| Unemployment Compensation Payments | +1 |
| The adjustment is for projected changes in the costs of unemployment compensation claims to be paid to the Department of Labor, Federal Employees Compensation Account, in the Unemployment Trust Fund, pursuant to Public Law 96-499. | |
| Rental Payments | +295 |
| The adjustment is for changes in the costs payable to General Services Administration (GSA) and others resulting from changes in rates for office and non-office space as estimated by GSA, as well as the rental costs of other currently occupied space. These costs include building security; in the case of GSA space, these are paid to Department of Homeland Security (DHS). Costs of mandatory office relocations, i.e. relocations in cases where due to external events there is no alternative but to vacate the currently occupied space, are also included. | |

| Total, Fixed Costs and Related Changes in 2015 | +1,462 |
|---|---|

# FY 2015 PERFORMANCE BUDGET
Bureau of Ocean Energy Management
*Renewable Energy*

## Table 11: Renewable Energy Budget Summary

| | | 2013 Actual | 2014 Enacted | Fixed Costs (+/-) | Program Changes (+/-) | 2015 Request | Change from 2014 (+/-) |
|---|---|---|---|---|---|---|---|
| **Renewable Energy** | ($000) | 18,537 | 23,656 | +65 | -617 | 23,104 | -552 |
| | FTE | 47 | 47 | | | 47 | - |

## SUMMARY OF PROGRAM CHANGES

| Program Changes from 2014 Enacted | Amount ($000) | FTE |
|---|---|---|
| Programmatic Reduction | -617 | - |
| **Total Program Changes** | **-617** | **-** |

The FY 2015 President's Budget request for BOEM's Renewable Energy program is $23.1 million and 47 FTE, a net decrease of -$552,000 from the 2014 enacted level. This change is comprised of an increase in fixed costs of $65,000 and a programmatic reduction of $617,000.

**Programmatic Reduction (-$617,000; 0 FTE).** In order to support BOEM's highest priority needs in FY 2015, the Bureau is proposing to reduce programmatic funding for renewable energy activities and to realize additional savings by further implementing administrative restrictions on travel, training, and the filling of lower priority positions, similar to the measures taken during FY 2013.

## PROGRAM OVERVIEW

The Outer Continental Shelf has significant potential as a source of new domestic energy generation from renewable energy resources. Section 388 of the Energy Policy Act of 2005 gave the Secretary of the Interior the authority to issue leases, easements, and rights-of-way on the OCS for activities that produce or support production, transportation, or transmission of energy from sources other than oil and gas. Section 388 also authorized the Secretary to permit OCS activities that repurpose facilities currently or previously used for activities authorized under the OCS Lands Act. Renewable energy and alternate use projects may include wind, wave energy, and ocean current projects, as well as projects that make alternative use of existing oil and gas platforms in Federal waters.

**Offshore commercial wind-powered electricity generator**

In 2009, President Obama and Secretary Salazar announced the promulgation of BOEM's renewable energy regulations. These regulations established a framework for the Renewable Energy Program's planning, leasing and operations authorization processes that would allow for orderly, safe and environmentally responsible OCS renewable energy development and provide for a fair return for use of OCS lands. Also in 2009, the Minerals Management Service and the Federal Energy Regulatory Commission (FERC) signed a memorandum of understanding that provided for joint regulation of potential OCS wave and ocean current projects. The agreement recognizes BOEM as having exclusive jurisdiction with regard to production, transportation, or transmission of energy from non-hydrokinetic renewable energy projects on the OCS as well as issuing leases, easements, and rights-of-way for hydrokinetic projects. According to the terms of the agreement, FERC has exclusive jurisdiction to issue licenses and exemptions for OCS hydrokinetic projects. Following the reorganization of the MMS, the Renewable Energy Program under BOEM continues to support these activities on the OCS.

Since the regulations were put in place, BOEM has worked diligently to support the Administration's goal of promoting renewable energy development and respond to the rapidly growing state interests in pursuing offshore wind and wave development. To date, BOEM has issued five commercial wind energy leases offshore (Massachusetts, Delaware, Rhode Island, and Virginia); conducted two competitive wind energy lease sales for areas offshore Rhode Island, Massachusetts, and Virginia; and approved the construction operations plan for the Cape Wind project offshore Massachusetts. Additionally, BOEM has initiated auction planning for areas offshore Maryland, New Jersey, and Massachusetts, and is in the early planning stages for areas offshore North Carolina and New York. Unsolicited requests for research leases off Virginia and Florida and transmission rights-of-way off Rhode Island and on the Mid Atlantic are also being processed. On the West Coast, BOEM has established renewable energy task forces to consider areas offshore Oregon and Hawaii, and in September 2013, issued a call for information and nominations to gauge interest in an area offshore Oregon for which BOEM received an unsolicited application. Additionally offshore Oregon, BOEM is processing an unsolicited request for an OCS hydrokinetic research lease.

In the foreseeable future, BOEM anticipates development of renewable energy on the OCS from three general sources:

1. *Offshore Wind Energy.* Offshore wind turbines are being used in a number of countries to harness the energy of the moving air over the oceans and convert it to electricity. Offshore winds tend to flow at higher sustained speeds than onshore winds, making turbines more efficient. As seen in Figure 2, offshore wind speeds along the Atlantic and

Pacific coasts indicate those areas as having the greatest potential for offshore wind energy production.

**Figure 2: Offshore Wind Speeds in Coastal Areas**

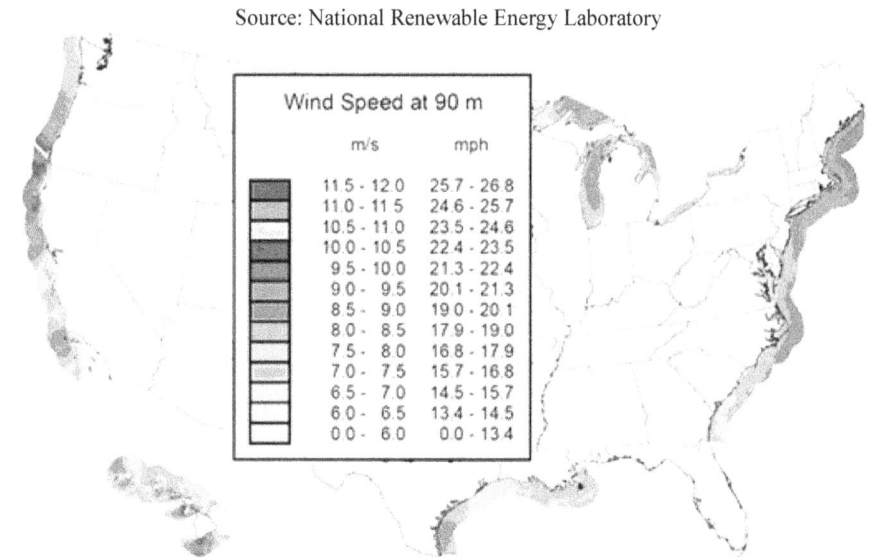

Source: National Renewable Energy Laboratory

In 2011, the Department of the Interior and the Department of Energy announced a National Offshore Wind Strategy with a scenario for achieving ten gigawatts of wind capacity in the OCS and Great Lakes by 2020 (potential renewable energy development in the Great Lakes is regulated by the Army Corps of Engineers). Winds offshore the Atlantic coast alone have the technical potential to produce an estimated 1,000 gigawatts of energy; wind offshore the Hawaiian Islands is considered to be an option for addressing the cost of electricity in Hawaii, which has the highest electricity costs in America (Hawaii is almost exclusively dependent on oil/gas transported to the islands aboard ships and barges). Additionally, developers are proposing to use areas offshore Oregon to demonstrate new technologies to support deepwater wind energy generation. The strategy seeks to harness a small portion of this potential by driving down the cost of offshore wind production to make it competitive with other electricity generating sources.

2. *Ocean Wave Energy (Hydrokinetic).* There is tremendous energy in ocean waves, and technology and project developers are evaluating existing and developing wave technology to garner this energy. Wave power devices extract energy directly from the surface motion of ocean waves. A variety of technologies have been proposed to garner that energy, and some of the more promising designs are undergoing demonstration testing. West Coast States (California, Oregon and Washington) and Hawaii have all received attention from developers as sites for wave energy parks.

3. *Ocean Current Energy (Hydrokinetic).* Ocean currents also contain an enormous amount of energy that can be garnered and converted to a usable form. Some of the ocean currents on the OCS are the Gulf Stream, Florida Straits Current, and California Current.

At this time, the area with the greatest potential for ocean current energy development is the Florida coast. Technology is still at an early stage of development, but it is likely that submerged water turbines similar to wind turbines may be employed to extract energy from ocean currents in the future. BOEM is currently considering a proposal for a research lease focused on hydrokinetic technology testing.

## RENEWABLE ENERGY AUTHORIZATION PROCESS

Current renewable energy activities on the OCS are focused on wind projects. Under the renewable energy regulations, the identification of Wind Energy Areas, the issuance of leases and subsequent review of energy development activities on the OCS is a staged decision-making process. BOEM's renewable energy leasing process is comprised of four distinct phases: (1) planning and analysis; (2) lease, right-of-way grant, or right-of-use and easement grant issuance; (3) site assessment; and (4) construction and operations. BOEM involves other Federal agencies (Department of Defense, U.S. Fish and Wildlife Service, U.S. Coast Guard, etc.) and state, local and Tribal governments throughout all phases of renewable energy development. Figure 3 below outlines BOEM's process for authorizing wind energy leases.

**Figure 3: Phases of BOEM's Offshore Wind Energy Authorization Process**

| Planning and Analysis | Lease or Grant | Site Assessment | Construction and Operations |
|---|---|---|---|
| • BOEM publishes Call for Information and Nominations | • BOEM determines whether Competitive Interest exists | • Lessee conducts site characterization studies | • Lessee may conduct additional site characterization |
| • BOEM identifies priority Wind Energy Areas (WEAs) offshore. WEAs are locations that appear most suitable for wind energy development | • *If Competitive Interest exists*, BOEM notifies the public and developers of its intent to lease through Sale Notices before holding a lease or grant auction | • Lessee submits Site Assessment Plan (SAP) | • Lessee submits Construction and Operations Plan (COP) |
| • Processes unsolicited application for lease or grant | • *If Competitive Interest does not exist*, BOEM negotiates a lease or grant (note: issuance may be combined with plan approval) | • BOEM conducts environmental and technical reviews of SAP, eventually deciding to approve, approve with modification, or disapprove the SAP | • BOEM conducts environmental and technical reviews of COP, eventually deciding to approve, approve with modification, or disapprove the COP |
| • BOEM may prepare an Environmental Assessment for Lease Issuance and Site Assessment Activities | | • If approved, lessee assesses site (usually with meteorological tower(s) and/or buoy(s)) | • If approved, lessee builds wind facility |

**Intergovernmental Task Force Engagement**

The Planning and Analysis phase seeks to identify suitable areas for wind energy leasing consideration through collaborative, consultative, and analytical processes that engage stakeholders, tribes, and state and Federal agencies. In this phase, BOEM conducts environmental compliance reviews and consultations with Tribes, states, and natural resource agencies.

The Lease and Grant phase results in the issuance of a commercial wind energy lease or right-of-way grant for energy transmission projects. Right-of-way grants authorize the holder to install on the OCS cables, pipelines and associated facilities that involve the transportation or transmission of electricity or other energy products from renewable energy projects. Leases and grants may be issued either through a competitive or noncompetitive process. A commercial lease gives the lessee the exclusive right to subsequently seek BOEM approval for the development of the leasehold. The lease does not provide the lessee the right to construct any facilities; rather, the lease provides the right to use the leased area to develop its plans, which must be approved by BOEM before the lessee can move on to the next stage of the process.

The Site Assessment phase includes the submission of a site assessment plan, which contains the lessee's detailed proposal for the construction of a meteorological tower and/or the installation of meteorological buoys on the leasehold to conduct site characterization studies. The lessee's site assessment plan must be approved by BOEM before it conducts these "site assessment" activities on the leasehold. BOEM may approve, approve with modification, or disapprove a lessee's site assessment plan. It is during this phase that the lessee would conduct site characterization surveys to support the development of future plans.

The Construction and Operations phase consists of the submission of a construction and operations plan, a detailed plan for the construction and operation of a wind energy project on the lease. BOEM requires a general activities plan, similar to a construction operations plan, for facilities constructed under a limited lease or right-of-way. BOEM conducts environmental and technical reviews of these plans and decides whether to approve, approve with modification, or disapprove the plan. At the end of the lease or grant term, the developer must decommission facilities in compliance with BOEM regulations.

> BOEM has established 12 intergovernmental task forces to enable representatives from state, local, and tribal governments and other Federal agencies to provide meaningful input into the OCS renewable energy planning process.

## PLANNING AND ANALYSIS

To help inform BOEM's planning and program decision-making processes, BOEM has established intergovernmental task forces in states where the Governor contacted BOEM to express interest in development of offshore renewable energy. Each task force collects and shares information for all stakeholders, including BOEM, for use in its decision-making process. BOEM intergovernmental task forces have been established in Maine, Massachusetts, Rhode Island, New York, New Jersey, Delaware, Maryland, Virginia, North Carolina, South Carolina, Oregon and Hawaii. Task forces have been extremely productive and have helped identify areas of significant promise and interest for offshore development, in addition to providing early identification and steps toward resolution of potential conflicts. BOEM will continue to respond to state interest in task forces along the East Coast (Florida) as well as the West Coast.

> ➤ **Identification of Wind Energy Areas**

A key element of the Planning and Analysis stage is the identification and refinement of Wind Energy Areas, which are areas on the OCS that appear to be particularly suitable for renewable energy development due to fewer potential multiple-use and environmental conflicts, such as conflicts from commercial vessel traffic or fisheries, and feeding or calving areas for endangered species. Through consultation with BOEM's intergovernmental task forces and its Call for Information and Nominations (Call) process, BOEM has identified Wind Energy Areas on the OCS offshore Rhode Island, Massachusetts, New Jersey, Delaware, Maryland, and Virginia. In FY 2014, BOEM expects to identify additional areas offshore North Carolina and New York; in FY 2015 BOEM expects to identify areas offshore South Carolina. These Wind Energy and Call areas are shown in the map below.

**Figure 4: Identified Wind Energy and Call Areas along the Atlantic Coast**

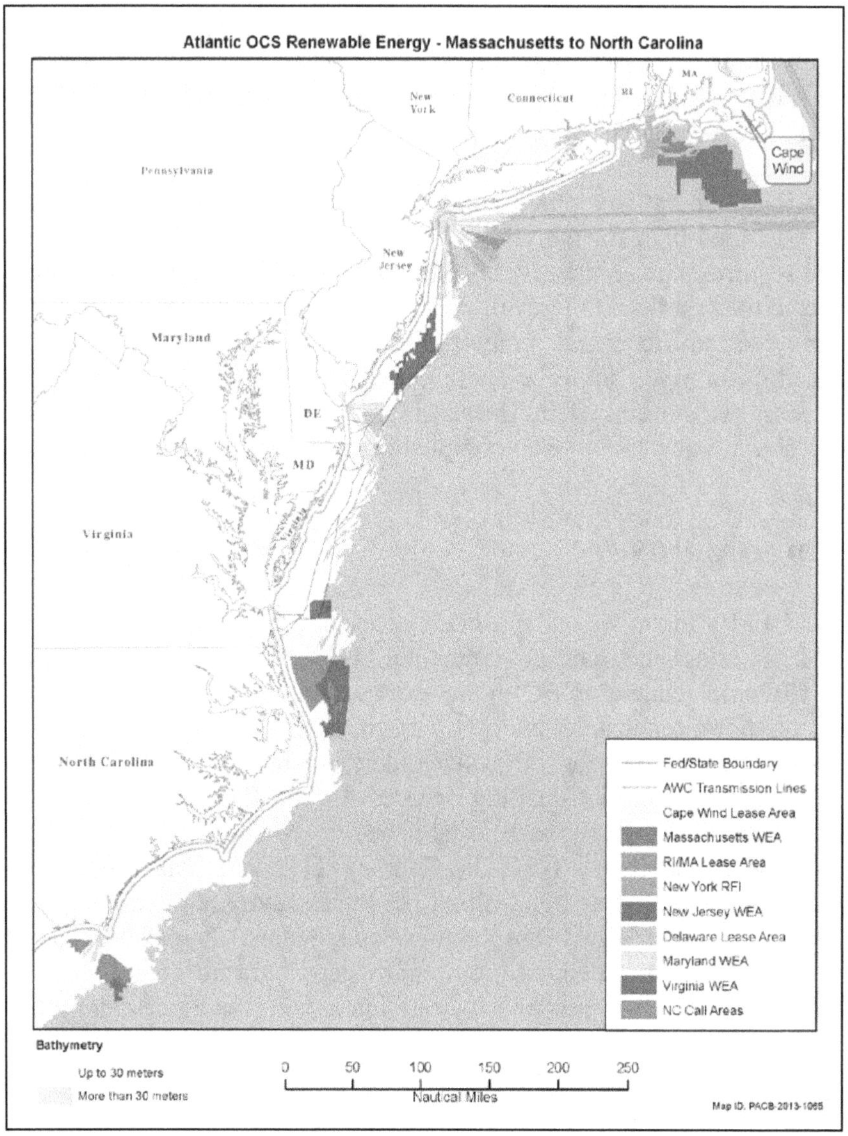

## LEASE AND GRANT ISSUANCE

As required by the Energy Policy Act of 2005, BOEM will issue a renewable energy lease or grant on a competitive basis unless it determines that no competitive interest exists in obtaining that lease or grant. To issue competitive renewable energy leases and grants, BOEM will hold an auction, and the lease or grant is awarded to the highest bidder. In contrast, the noncompetitive process takes the form of a negotiation between BOEM and the one developer. In either case, the developer must be qualified to hold an OCS lease or grant and submit and receive approval of appropriate plans (or FERC license applications for marine hydrokinetic projects) prior to moving forward with its proposed activities.

> The three commercial wind leases BOEM issued in FY 2013 cover over 277,000 acres on the OCS and, if fully developed, could provide enough energy to power 1.7 million homes.

➢ **Commercial Leasing on the Atlantic OCS**

As a result of collaboration and coordination with intergovernmental task forces and outreach efforts with relevant stakeholders, BOEM's Renewable Energy Program has made significant progress in its planning and leasing process to date. As of November 2013, BOEM has issued five commercial wind leases, including the following:

- In 2010, BOEM issued a commercial wind energy lease for the Cape Wind Energy Project offshore Massachusetts.

- In 2012, BOEM issued a commercial wind energy lease to Bluewater Wind Delaware, LLC for a project proposed offshore Delaware.

- In 2013, BOEM issued three commercial wind energy leases, including two in the Wind Energy Area offshore Rhode Island/Massachusetts, and another offshore Virginia.

BOEM anticipates issuing three additional commercial wind energy leases during FY 2014 and another six commercial leases during FY 2015.

Prior to issuing commercial wind energy leases, BOEM conducts a review of reasonably foreseeable impacts of associated site characterization surveys and subsequent site assessment activities. For example, BOEM's environmental assessment for the Wind Energy Areas offshore New Jersey, Delaware, Maryland, and Virginia supported the issuance of leases offshore Delaware and Virginia, and will allow for lease sales for areas offshore Maryland and New Jersey to occur in FY 2014. BOEM prepared a similar environmental assessment prior to the Rhode Island lease sale, and both documents resulted in Findings of No Significant Impact, an analysis concluding the action does not have significant impact on the environment.

➢ **Limited and Research Leasing on the Atlantic OCS**

In November 2007, the former MMS established an interim policy as a measure to jumpstart resource data collection and technology testing activities on the OCS prior to the promulgation of final regulations. BOEM's policy allows for limited leasing, resource data collection, and technology testing activities. A limited lease is a lease with terms and conditions which allows a person to conduct activities on the OCS that support the production of energy but do not result in the production of electricity or other energy product for sale, distribution, or other commercial use exceeding a limit specified in the lease. These limited leases have a five year term, require fee payment and provide no subsequent rights to commercial development. To date, BOEM has issued four such limited leases, three offshore New Jersey and one offshore Delaware. As a requirement of these leases, the lessee must submit for BOEM review a project plan that provides details on fabrication methods, engineering specifications, and safety systems for any facility to be installed in Federal waters. Two lessees have deployed meteorological buoys off the coast of New Jersey, and these two leases are set to expire in November 2014. The other two leases were relinquished in 2012.

BOEM anticipates issuing three limited leases during FY 2014, including those for projects proposed offshore Georgia and Florida.

- **Georgia**: On April 7, 2011, Southern Company submitted an Interim Policy lease application for the leasing of a three-block area on the OCS offshore Georgia for offshore renewable energy resource assessment activities. BOEM published a notice of intent to prepare an environmental assessment in the *Federal Register* in the first quarter of FY 2013. In FY 2014, BOEM will publish the environmental assessment and initiate associated consultations.

- **Florida**: In August 2011, Florida Atlantic University submitted its final application to BOEM for a lease to conduct marine hydrokinetic technology testing. In April 2012, BOEM published an environmental assessment for public review that considers the environmental impacts of the University's proposed project, which would entail the installation and testing of submerged turbine generators. To address the comments received, BOEM published a revised environmental assessment in August 2013, and as a result of the analysis in the revised environmental assessment, issued a Finding of No Significant Impact for the project. In FY 2014, BOEM will develop potential lease terms for the project.

During FY 2012, BOEM received an unsolicited application for a research lease from the Virginia Department of Mines, Minerals and Energy, proposing to install meteorological towers to facilitate wind resource assessment within the Virginia Wind Energy Area. Research leases support the future production, transportation, or transmission of renewable energy and are only available for state and Federal government entities, require no fees and have a negotiated lease term that could be unlimited. Subsequently, BOEM sought public input on the research proposal and its potential environmental consequences and also determined, based on the responses, that there was no competitive interest in the project. Later that year, BOEM received a second application, also from Virginia, requesting another lease area outside of the western boundary of the Virginia Wind Energy Area to install two six-megawatts, grid-connected wind turbines as a demonstration project. BOEM determined once again there was no competitive interest in the area where the Commonwealth proposed to conduct activities. The two determinations of no competitive interest clear the way for BOEM to proceed with the noncompetitive research lease process for both of the state-proposed projects.

➢ **Commercial Leasing in the Pacific Region**

In the Pacific Region, BOEM has received interest in commercial leases for wind and wave projects. As of the first quarter of FY 2014, BOEM has received a commercial wind lease request from Principle Power Incorporated for the WindFloat Pacific project offshore Coos Bay, Oregon. BOEM has determined there is no competitive interest in the requested area and is moving forward with the noncompetitive lease process. In January 2013, BOEM received two draft commercial lease application requests for an area on the OCS offshore the island of Oahu in Hawaii. Both lease requests are considered draft requests pending the finalization of the Department of Defense (DOD) assessment of offshore Oahu. Both project developers plan to submit formal lease requests to BOEM if DOD determines any of the technically feasible offshore wind development areas are compatible with national security and military operations. The final DOD assessment is expected in FY 2014.

Prior to issuing commercial wind energy leases, BOEM conducts environmental reviews of the lease areas. BOEM plans to conduct an environmental review of the WindFloat Pacific project prior to making a decision on lease issuance in the first quarter of FY 2016. BOEM may also conduct an environmental review for lease issuance offshore Oahu, depending on the final DOD assessment.

➢ **Research Leasing in the Pacific Region**

In November 2013, BOEM received a research lease request from the Northwest National Marine Renewable Energy Center, the research center at Oregon State University, for the Pacific Marine Energy Center-South Energy Test Site project. The project is a grid-connected wave energy test site proposed on the OCS offshore Newport, Oregon. BOEM expects to publish a Request for Competitive Interest in the *Federal Register* in 2014. Since the project is a wave energy test facility requiring a FERC license, BOEM plans to collaborate with FERC on the environmental review of the proposal prior to making a leasing decision in FY 2016.

➢ **Right-of-Way Grants**

BOEM has the authority to issue right-of-way grants that allow developers to build electricity transmission lines that connect renewable energy installations to the onshore electrical grid. During FY 2012, BOEM initiated two right-of-way grant processes. BOEM published two requests for competitive interest in the *Federal Register* for a proposed transmission backbone project that would run from Virginia to New York (Atlantic Wind Connection) and a cable project that would support a wind project to be located in Rhode Island State waters (Block Island Transmission System). BOEM expects additional unsolicited applications for right-of-way grants in the near future, and the Bureau anticipates making decisions on right-of-way grants for the Block Island Transmission System offshore Rhode Island in FY 2014 and the Atlantic Wind Connection in FY 2015.

BOEM expects to receive requests for right-of-way grants in the future, including one to allow transmission through Federal waters between the islands of Oahu and Maui in Hawaii. One component of the state's Hawaii Clean Energy Initiative is an inter-island cable to transmit power from future energy-producing installations on various islands to Oahu, the main demand center. A portion of this cable will be on the OCS. BOEM is working with Hawaii and the Department of Energy on programmatic issues associated with the inter-island cable as part of a programmatic environmental impact statement on Hawaii wind energy. BOEM anticipates receiving a right-of-way/right-of-use grant request for a Hawaii inter-island cable as early as FY 2014, with a final decision on the grant request by FY 2016.

## ➢ Payments

As required by the Energy Policy Act of 2005, BOEM has established payment terms to ensure fair return to the U.S. Treasury for the rights conveyed by OCS renewable energy leases and grants. All lessees and grantees must pay rent, and lessees must pay an operating fee in lieu of rent when commercial electrical generation commences. The operating fee is based on the installed capacity of the wind turbine generators. In FY 2013, $425,160 in rent payments were collected on OCS renewable energy leases. BOEM estimates rent payments of more than $1.5 million in FY 2014 and $4.5 million in FY 2015, in addition to bonus bids that may be collected from lease sales held in those years.

## ➢ Coordination and Collaboration

In addition to the establishment of BOEM intergovernmental task forces, the Department also established memoranda of understanding relevant to offshore renewable energy coordination with the Department of Energy, BSEE, the U.S. Fish and Wildlife Service, the Department of Defense, the U.S. Coast Guard, and the National Oceanic and Atmospheric Administration.

BOEM and FERC responsibilities intersect for marine hydrokinetic projects, with BOEM issuing commercial marine hydrokinetic leases and FERC issuing licenses for construction and operation of these projects. The agencies have worked together to achieve efficiencies for both the agencies and potential applicants. To that end, the two agencies signed a memorandum of understanding in April 2009, issued joint guidelines for potential marine hydrokinetic developers later that year, and updated those guidelines in July 2012.

## RESEARCH, DATA COLLECTION AND STAKEHOLDER ENGAGEMENT

BOEM's Renewable Energy Program is supported by a substantial investment in research, data collection and stakeholder engagement. The areas that are appropriate for renewable energy development have likely never been studied for such development; in some cases, there is a dearth of information about the physical and biological environment. BOEM has worked closely with a broad spectrum of agencies, universities and stakeholders to identify the critical data gaps and independently or through partnerships sought to fund studies through its Environmental Studies Program. To benefit from lessons learned, BOEM has also reached out to European countries with more mature renewable energy programs.

The continued need to pursue information to ensure access to the OCS for renewable energy development and to ensure that such development is environmentally appropriate is a high priority for BOEM. BOEM's Environmental Studies Program has broadened its research since the Energy Policy Act of 2005 gave BOEM the authority to develop renewable energy resources on the OCS. This research augments what had been done previously for offshore oil and gas and marine minerals, but with an extra interest in renewable energy applications. To ensure full environmental review, BOEM has spent close to $40 million since FY 2007 on environmental studies that address renewable energy issues, either solely or in addition to other OCS resource activities. Efforts funded through BOEM's Environmental Studies Program are described in more detail in the Environmental Programs activity.

➢ **Data Collection through Cooperative and Interagency Agreements**

In accordance with the OCS Lands Act, BOEM is working cooperatively with states by leveraging funds to collect important information about the offshore environment that meets both the needs of BOEM and the states. In FY 2013, BOEM continued or executed the following cooperative agreements with state partners, through matching funds, to inform future planning and decision-making:

> As part of its outreach efforts, BOEM has held targeted workshops focused on key stakeholder areas of interest including: site visualization simulations, renewable energy technologies, and mitigation measures to address potential conflicts between fishing and wind energy development.

- The Commonwealth of Virginia continuing support to collect baseline information about the surface and near surface geology of the Virginia Wind Energy Area;

- The Commonwealth of Massachusetts continuing support for the collection of baseline information on marine mammals, sea turtles, and birds in the Massachusetts and Rhode Island/ Massachusetts Wind Energy Area;

- The University of Rhode Island to support the collection of information about lobsters in the Rhode Island/ Massachusetts and Massachusetts Wind Energy Areas; and

- The University of North Carolina - Chapel Hill for fishing stakeholder meetings to identify access routes and fishing grounds in the three North Carolina Call Areas and hard bottom habitat surveys in Call Area Wilmington East to identify artificial reefs and archaeological sites.

➢ **Renewable Energy Workshops and Conferences**

Stakeholder engagement is integral to BOEM's renewable energy planning and leasing efforts. Following are some highlights of recent outreach events.

- **OCS Renewable Energy Studies Workshop.** BOEM's Pacific Region held an OCS Marine Renewable Energy Environmental Science Conference at the beginning of FY 2013 to identify completed and ongoing research that addresses environmental questions associated with wave and wind energy development in the Pacific Northwest; to synthesize new research and existing information and distill it into products that agencies and resource managers can use; and to identify and prioritize study gaps of the technologies or potentially affected systems that can be used for scientists, managers, and funders to focus future research efforts. The conference report was published in April 2013.

- **Offshore Wind Energy Development Site Assessment and Characterization Workshop.** In February 2013, BOEM hosted a workshop titled: "Offshore Wind Energy Development Site Assessment and Characterization: Evaluation of the Current Status and European Experience." This workshop brought together European experts to further inform the development of site assessment and characterization guidelines for surveys of avian species, benthic habitat and archaeological resources.

- **Pacific Region Workshops.** BOEM held public workshops in both Oregon and Hawaii in FY 2013. These workshops were conducted under a contract with the Department of Energy's National Renewable Energy Laboratory and provided information on technologies specific to the Region (floating wind turbines in Hawaii and marine hydrokinetic and wind in Oregon). An additional public workshop may be conducted in FY 2014 due to increased interest expressed in offshore renewable energy development in California.

- **Fishing/Offshore Wind Mitigation Measures Development Workshops.** BOEM is developing best management practices and mitigation measures for analysis and decision-making under the National Environmental Policy Act associated with wind energy development and activities on the OCS as they relate to interaction with commercial and recreational fishing practices. To address future conflicts between fishing and wind projects on the OCS, BOEM sought input from commercial and recreational fishing industries, as well as fisheries management agencies and scientists, relative to proposed offshore wind energy development. In order to effectively engage the fishing industry and its many fisheries and technologies, as well as wind energy developers, eight stakeholder workshops were held from October 2012 to February 2013 from Maine through North Carolina to allow for dialogue among the parties. The Fishing/Offshore Wind Mitigation Measures Development Workshops contract resulted in a draft report that was posted to BOEM's website in November 2013, with comments on the draft report requested by February 14, 2014. During the comment period BOEM supported a Mid-Atlantic Fishery Management Council workshop to get additional feedback on the best management practices with additional insights provided by three commercial fishermen from the UK. BOEM is compiling the comments and anticipates the final document being available in late spring 2014.

- **North Carolina Visual Simulations and Open Houses.** BOEM collaborated with the National Park Service to create state of the art visual simulations of a wind energy facility offshore North Carolina. These computer simulations provide spatially accurate and realistic visual simulations of offshore wind energy facilities within a specific area on the OCS and enable BOEM and its stakeholders to visualize what the facilities will look like at different distances and with different configurations. In August 2013, BOEM held Visual Simulation Open Houses in North Carolina to provide an opportunity to review the results, which focused on locations within the Cape Hatteras and Cape Lookout National Seashores.

### ➤ Guidelines for Developers and Applicants

In FY 2013, BOEM posted guidelines for providing survey information on avian resources, spatial data, benthic habitats, fish, marine mammals, and sea turtles on the Atlantic OCS. The purpose is to clarify and provide a general understanding of the information that BOEM requires in order to adequately address the impacts of offshore renewable energy projects to the environment. The guidelines were developed with input from FWS, NOAA and the Marine Mammal Commission.

### ➤ Technology Assessment and Research Studies

Recent projects continue to build on the lessons learned from developers of commercial wind projects offshore in Europe while focusing on the unique operating environment of the U.S. Outer Continental Shelf. International structural design standards have been reviewed and research gaps have been identified that include the anticipated effects of hurricanes and open-ocean breaking waves, as well as the structural integrity of floating wind turbines under reasonably-foreseeable ocean conditions. Much is known about the meteorological and oceanographic conditions in the Gulf of Mexico, but this data needs to be obtained in both the Atlantic and Pacific regions to ensure that these new structures are designed to the appropriate parameters. Studies planned for FY 2014 include: Cable Spacing, Offshore Substation Design, Development of "Regional" Metocean Conditions for individual Wind Energy Areas on the Atlantic seaboard, and Development of Hazard Curves for Wind Energy Areas off the Atlantic seaboard.

### ➤ Outlook on Renewable Energy

Through detailed planning and analysis and partnerships with other governmental agencies and stakeholders, BOEM has advanced the Renewable Energy Program nationwide and will continue to do so in 2015. Offshore wind leasing activities, including commercial leases, research leases and right-of-way grants, have increased, contributing to meeting the Administration's goal of promoting clean energy development. BOEM continues to demonstrate science-based decision-making by initiating and funding research studies. The studies directly benefit BOEM, other energy and mineral programs, renewable energy stakeholders and individual states. State interest in pursuing offshore renewable energy development is readily apparent in the increased involvement by the states through BOEM's intergovernmental renewable energy task forces. BOEM anticipates the Renewable Energy Program will continue to grow and is prepared to support this valuable effort in response to the Nation's energy needs.

*This page intentionally left blank.*

# 2015 PERFORMANCE BUDGET
## Bureau of Ocean Energy Management
### *Conventional Energy*

**Table 12: Conventional Energy Budget Summary**

| | | 2013 Actual | 2014 Enacted | Fixed Costs (+/-) | Program Changes (+/-) | 2015 Request | Change from 2014 (+/-) |
|---|---|---|---|---|---|---|---|
| **Conventional Energy** | ($000) | 46,115 | 49,441 | +353 | -161 | 49,633 | +192 |
| *[TIMS]* | | *[5,614]* | *[5,737]* | - | *[+98]* | *[5,835]* | *[+98]* |
| | FTE | 261 | 268 | | | 268 | - |

## SUMMARY OF PROGRAM CHANGES

| Program Changes from 2014 Enacted | Amount ($000) | FTE |
|---|---|---|
| Programmatic Reduction | -161 | - |
| **Total Program Changes** | **-161** | **-** |

The FY 2015 President's Budget request for BOEM's Conventional Energy budget activity is $49.6 million and 268 FTE, a net increase of +$192,000 from the 2014 enacted level. This change is comprised of an increase for fixed costs of $353,000 and a programmatic reduction of $161,000.

**Programmatic Reduction (-$161,000; 0 FTE).** In order to support BOEM's highest priority needs in FY 2015, the Bureau is proposing to reduce programmatic funding for conventional energy activities and realize additional savings by further implementing administrative restrictions on travel, training, and the filling of lower priority positions, similar to the measures taken during FY 2013.

## PROGRAM OVERVIEW

BOEM manages access to and fair return for the energy and mineral resources of the Outer Continental Shelf to help meet the energy demands and mineral needs of the Nation, while also balancing such access with the protection of the human, marine, and coastal environments. As the Nation's offshore energy and mineral resource manager, BOEM administers a comprehensive, progressive cycle of analyses to provide the key information necessary for decisions about where, whether and when offshore energy and mineral development can or should occur. BOEM's responsibilities are broad, beginning with identifying and calculating appropriate boundaries and legal descriptions; identifying, inventorying, and assessing the

Nation's offshore energy and mineral endowment; developing a transparent, systematic, and comprehensive schedule for OCS oil and gas resource offerings; developing appropriate financial terms to ensure the Nation receives fair market value for its OCS resources; and carefully reviewing requests for approval of comprehensive, detailed industry plans to explore, develop and produce leased resources.

BOEM conducts a range of activities in order to successfully manage OCS oil and gas resources. A key initial step is the assessment of undiscovered technically recoverable oil and gas resources of the Nation's OCS. The objective of this assessment is to identify areas on the OCS that offer the highest potential for the occurrence of oil and natural gas resources that may be considered for development. BOEM utilizes the most up-to-date resource assessment information in the preparation of a five-year schedule of proposed lease sales, which includes establishing the size, timing, and location of oil and gas lease sales and balancing the potential for environmental impacts, discovery of oil and gas, views of affected states, and impacts on the coastal zone. BOEM also researches, analyzes, and establishes lease terms and conditions that foster competition and ensure receipt of fair market value for the Nation's OCS resources.

To inform oil and gas resource assessments, BOEM authorizes industry to collect geological and geophysical (G&G) data, which BOEM then acquires. Analysis of G&G data allows BOEM to estimate existing and likely to be produced resources and evaluate market forces to forecast industry activity levels in a particular region. This supports BOEM's fair market value analysis and determinations of the adequacy of high bids received for individual tracts offered in a lease sale.

BOEM also is responsible for the management of all OCS minerals other than oil and gas and plays a unique role in providing coastal resources protection and sustainable management through the conveyance of sand and gravel resources.

As of January 2014, BOEM administers 6,365 active oil and gas leases on nearly 36 million OCS acres. Production from these leases generates billions of dollars in revenue for the Federal Treasury and state governments while supporting tens of thousands of jobs. In calendar year 2012, OCS leases provided 482 million barrels of oil and 1,585 billion cubic feet of natural gas, accounting for about 20 percent of domestic oil production and six percent of domestic natural gas production (source: http://www.data.bsee.gov/homepg/data_center/production/ocsprod.asp). Energy revenues generated from BOEM leasing actions and collected by the Office of Natural Resources Revenue (ONRR) are a significant source of revenue for the Federal Government.

## LEASING

BOEM's leasing and planning activities include preparing the Five Year OCS Oil and Gas Leasing Program, leasing marine minerals, mapping and surveying OCS boundaries, implementing the lease sale process, administering leases, and reviewing and approving exploration and development plans.

➢ **Five Year OCS Oil and Gas Leasing Program**

Under the OCS Lands Act, the Secretary of the Interior has the responsibility to "prepare and periodically revise, and maintain an oil and gas leasing program" in order to "best meet national energy needs" while still balancing other important factors. The Department must prepare a long-range program that indicates "as precisely as possible, the size, timing, and location" of Federal offshore oil and gas leasing activity to be considered for the five year period following its approval. The Five Year Program identifies the planning areas, which are delineated areas of leasing interest where potential leases may be offered, and establishes a schedule of potential lease sales over the five year period. Ultimately, the Five Year Program is designed to achieve the careful balance required under the OCS Lands Act. The identification and planning effort ensures that "management of the Outer Continental Shelf shall be conducted in a manner which considers economic, social, and environmental values of the renewable and nonrenewable resources contained in the Outer Continental Shelf, and the potential impact of oil and gas exploration on other resource values of the Outer Continental Shelf and the marine, coastal, and human environments." BOEM cooperates and/or consults with stakeholders (including Federal and state agencies, local communities, federally recognized tribes, private industry, and the public) to develop a program that offers access to those areas of the OCS with the most promising potential for development of oil and gas resources in an environmentally responsible manner.

The 2012-2017 Five Year Program, as approved by the Secretary in August 2012, schedules fifteen lease sales in six offshore planning areas with active leases and/or activity currently underway. During the course of this Program, these six planning areas are best situated to support lease sales with the potential to lead to responsible oil and gas exploration, development, and production. Twelve of the fifteen scheduled lease sales are within the Gulf of Mexico, which remains the area of greatest interest and known potential. This is also where the infrastructure supporting the oil and gas industry, including resources to respond in the event of an emergency, are the most mature and well developed. The Gulf of Mexico currently supplies approximately 20 percent of the Nation's oil production, and the Central and Western Gulf of Mexico remain the two offshore areas of highest resource potential and industry interest.

While the Five Year Program does not include any sales in the Alaska Region during FY 2015, there are two sales scheduled to take place during calendar year 2016: Chukchi Sea Sale 237 and Cook Inlet Sale 244. The preliminary processes for these two sales are well underway and are expected to continue as outlined in the Five Year Program. One sale is scheduled for calendar year 2017: the Beaufort Sea Sale 242. The process for this sale will be initiated during FY 2014. All three sales utilize the targeted leasing model described in the Five Year Program. The purpose of targeted leasing is to design potential lease sales in a manner that makes significant oil and gas resources available while minimizing conflicts in access to, use of, and management of the OCS, such as subsistence hunting and fishing and intrinsic environmental value, consistent with BOEM's mandate under the OCS Lands Act to balance social, economic, and environmental considerations. To achieve this goal, the targeted leasing model is designed to make certain determinations early in the sale process to identify the blocks within a planning area which are most suitable for leasing. The sale area is then defined before starting the draft environmental impact statement and environmental consultations, and further refined through the remaining steps of the sale process, as shown in Figure 5 below.

With respect to the Atlantic, the current Five Year Program does not include a scheduled sale in any Atlantic areas, but areas of the Atlantic will be considered for future Five Year Programs. BOEM is proceeding with a region-specific strategy to support future decision-making regarding whether – and, if so, where – potential offshore oil and gas lease sales in the Mid- and South Atlantic Planning Areas would be appropriate. In working toward the goal of supporting future decision making, BOEM recently completed a final programmatic environmental impact statement (EIS) relating to geologic and geophysical surveys in the Mid- and South Atlantic Planning Areas. The programmatic EIS will facilitate decision-making regarding new, responsible resource evaluation in areas where current estimates are based on older data collected in the 1970's and 1980's. Information garnered from any new G&G surveys will provide valuable data to inform the development and implementation of future Five Year Programs.

Additionally, BOEM will continue to work with the Department of Defense on complex issues relating to potential use conflicts in certain Atlantic OCS areas. In January 2013, BOEM and the Department of Defense signed a charter creating the "Interagency Working Group on South and Mid-Atlantic OCS Planning Areas Spatial Conflict Minimization" and the "Interagency Working Group on Passive Acoustic Monitoring in U.S. Atlantic OCS Waters." These groups are working to minimize potential conflicts in these areas when, and if, seismic surveying activities are approved.

The next Five Year Program is expected to encompass the 2017-2022 time period, beginning approximately in July 2017. Because of the complexity of the program development process, BOEM must begin planning for the next Program several years in advance. This includes an updated assessment of undiscovered technically recoverable oil and gas resources of the Nation's OCS, to be conducted in 2016.

The development of a Five Year Program begins with an initial request for information and results in a published proposed final program and environmental impact statement. Pursuant to the OCS Lands Act, BOEM consults with all interested parties throughout the process, with particular consideration given to suggestions of affected state Governors and interested Federal agencies.

**Figure 5: Five Year Program Development Process**

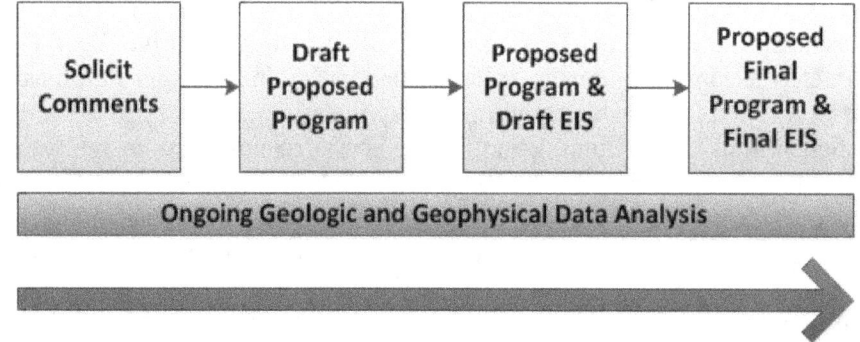

As a result of this necessary coordination of stakeholder input, the entire process to develop a Five Year Program normally takes approximately two and a half to three years. So while efforts to begin developing the next Five Year Program are already underway, FY 2015 will be a critical year for the development of the Program. Specifically, BOEM anticipates soliciting comments by issuing the initial Request for Information before the end of FY 2014.

➤ **Oil and Gas Lease Sales**

As of December 2013, three lease sales scheduled on the current Five Year Program have been held: Western Gulf of Mexico Sale 229 on November 28, 2012, Central Gulf of Mexico Sale 227 on March 20, 2013, and Western Gulf of Mexico Sale 233 on August 28, 2013. From these sales, BOEM issued 474 leases for bonus bids of over $1.4 billion. Twelve sales remain on the sale schedule through mid 2017. The next sales scheduled are Eastern Gulf of Mexico Sale 225 and Central Gulf of Mexico Sale 231, to be held concurrently in March 2014. Table 13 below shows the lease sales scheduled as part of the current Five Year Program. Upcoming sales are listed by calendar year.

**Table 13: Lease Sales in the 2012-2017 Five Year Program**

| Date of Sale | Area | Sale #* | Amt. High Bids Received |
|---|---|---|---|
| 11/28/2012 | Western Gulf of Mexico | 229 | $133,767,974 |
| 3/20/2013 | Central Gulf of Mexico | 227 | $1,214,675,536 |
| 8/28/2013 | Western Gulf of Mexico | 233 | $102,351,712 |
| 2014 | Eastern Gulf of Mexico** | 225 | - |
| 2014 | Central Gulf of Mexico | 231 | - |
| 2014 | Western Gulf of Mexico | 238 | - |
| 2015 | Central Gulf of Mexico | 235 | - |
| 2015 | Western Gulf of Mexico | 246 | - |
| 2016 | Eastern Gulf of Mexico | 226 | - |
| 2016 | Central Gulf of Mexico | 241 | - |
| 2016 | Chukchi Sea | 237 | - |
| 2016 | Western Gulf of Mexico | 248 | - |
| 2016 | Cook Inlet | 244 | - |
| 2017 | Central Gulf of Mexico | 247 | - |
| 2017 | Beaufort Sea | 242 | - |

*Numbers listed here are not in numerical order. Sale numbers are chosen as an administrative tool to identify individual proposals. Once a number has been assigned to a sale under a Draft Proposed Program, it cannot be reused in any subsequent revisions of that Five Year Program.

**Sales in Eastern Gulf of Mexico would only include those areas that are not currently subject to moratorium under Gulf of Mexico Energy Security Act.

## ➢ Lease Sale Planning Process

The lease sale planning process includes activities ranging from stakeholder outreach to environmental analyses to fulfilling numerous statutory considerations. BOEM conducts a detailed planning process for each lease sale specified in the Five Year Program. This may take two or more years, and thus, the lease sale planning process may start prior to the beginning of a new Five Year Program and multiple processes are running concurrently. These parallel planning steps allow BOEM to meet multiple overlapping regulatory requirements, including those of the OCS Lands Act, National Environmental Policy Act, and the Coastal Zone Management Act.

The first step in the sale process for an individual area is to publish a call for information and nominations (call) and a notice of intent to prepare an environmental impact statement (EIS). Subsequent steps include publishing the proposed and final notice of sale, providing consistency determinations and sale notifications to the affected states, and developing an environmental impact statement. An overview of the general process for conducting a lease sale is shown below in Figure 6. Although the basic requirements for lease sale planning are specified in the OCSLA and the Code of Federal Regulations (30 CFR 556), the specific timing and preliminary steps in the process may vary depending on the previous history of leasing within a sale area. For example, under the targeted leasing model for proposed sales in the Arctic OCS, BOEM may issue the call before the EIS notice of intent. Staggering these steps allows industry to indicate their interest in the specific portions of the sale area before BOEM proceeds further with the sale process. Other modifications to the sale process may be appropriate for future sales in different frontier areas.

**Figure 6: Planning for a Specific Lease Sale**

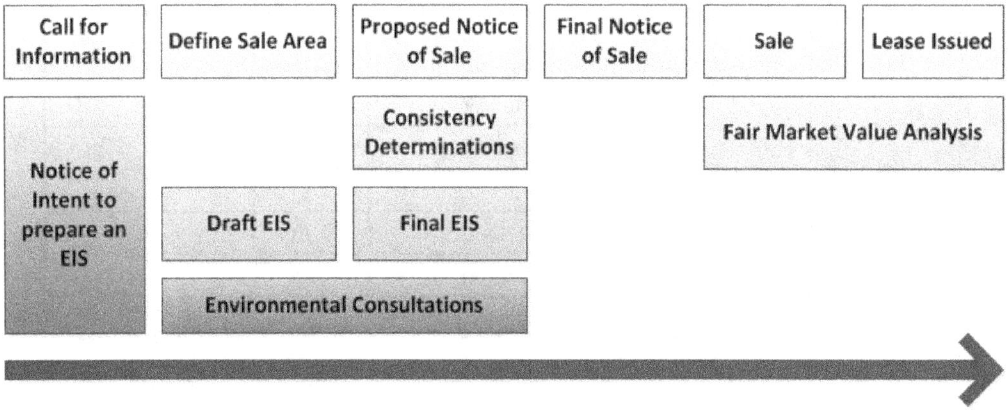

## ➢ Lease Administration

The lease administration process encompasses a set of discrete business processes, which manage a lease from inception to relinquishment, termination or expiration. Once the lease has been officially awarded, lease administration covers the legal modification of the lease contract, its supporting analysis, and services provided by BOEM under the lease contract. Also included within these processes, are the qualification of corporate entities and individuals before they can acquire properties or do business on the OCS, the review and acceptance of corporate mergers, corporate changes-of-name, and business conversions.

To improve efficiency within the Bureau and customer relations with industry users, in August 2012, BOEM implemented TIMS Web (TIMS refers to BOEM's Technical Information Management System). This new web-based tool allows oil and gas industry users to submit online requests for company, qualification, merger and bonding information for review and approval. TIMS Web was designed to help expedite the process and reduce errors through data validation of submitted documents and to improve operating efficiency with real-time access to industry information and data.

➤ **Financial Accountability and Risk Management**

As a steward of OCS resources, BOEM is charged with managing a variety of risks associated with offshore operations. Some of these risks are intrinsically related to financial assurance and loss prevention to the U.S. Government and the American taxpayer. BOEM is responsible for protecting the U.S. Government from incurring financial losses when an entity fails to meet its lease, grant, or permit obligations on the OCS. Lessees, grantees, and operators are required to decommission all structures and wells within one year of termination of the agreement under which they were installed or drilled. BOEM is responsible for ensuring that all entities performing activities under its jurisdiction provide or demonstrate adequate financial assurance to protect the U.S. Government from incurring any financial loss. Each lease, right-of-way, and right-of-use and easement on the OCS is reviewed to ensure that a lessee, operator, or holder has demonstrated adequate financial assurance that ensures the performance of all obligations, should the designated operator/holder or any of the lessees be unable to fulfill its lease requirements, including decommissioning and environmental remediation.

A recent self-analysis of BOEM's risk management strategy found deficiencies in efforts to shield taxpayers from existing financial risks. Beginning in FY 2014, BOEM will work to revise its risk management program to address this, as well as weaknesses identified by BOEM's 2007 and 2009 bonding program reviews. The reviews found limited financial risk assessment processes in place and a lack of Quality Assurance/Quality Control for associated data collection and maintenance procedures. BOEM will work to ensure that these weaknesses are corrected in order to incorporate project risk management practices that do not currently exist within the Bureau or the Department.

**PLANS**

Before approving any drilling activity on existing leases, BOEM conducts in-depth reviews and processes exploration plans, development and production plans, and development operation coordination documents for approval within required time frames to ensure that planned activities are conducted in accordance with applicable laws, regulations, and lease terms. BOEM works to ensure that the review process is rigorous, efficient, and transparent, while also being predictable to industry. For example, BOEM now designates specific plan coordinators to ensure consistency throughout the review process and is currently developing electronic systems to make the process more user-friendly and the status more transparent.

In conducting plan reviews, which include environmental analyses required by NEPA, BOEM examines a broad spectrum of issues and resources including shallow drilling hazards, resource conservation, supplemental bonding, worst case discharge analysis, air quality, water quality, archaeological concerns, environmental resource concerns, subsistence use concerns, and military and security issues.

These analyses provide information that is needed to support plan decisions, including the development of approval conditions to help protect the environment and facilitate multiple use of the OCS. BOEM's regional offices, working closely with the Office of Strategic Resources and the Office of Environmental Programs, coordinate and manage the plan review process between the Conventional Energy and Environmental Programs activities. BOEM also coordinates its review of plans with BSEE, as well as with states that have approved Coastal Zone Management Programs, and with other appropriate state and Federal agencies. Figure 7 and 8 show the typical process for reviewing and approving exploration and development plans.

**Figure 7: Processes for Development and Approval of Exploration Plans**

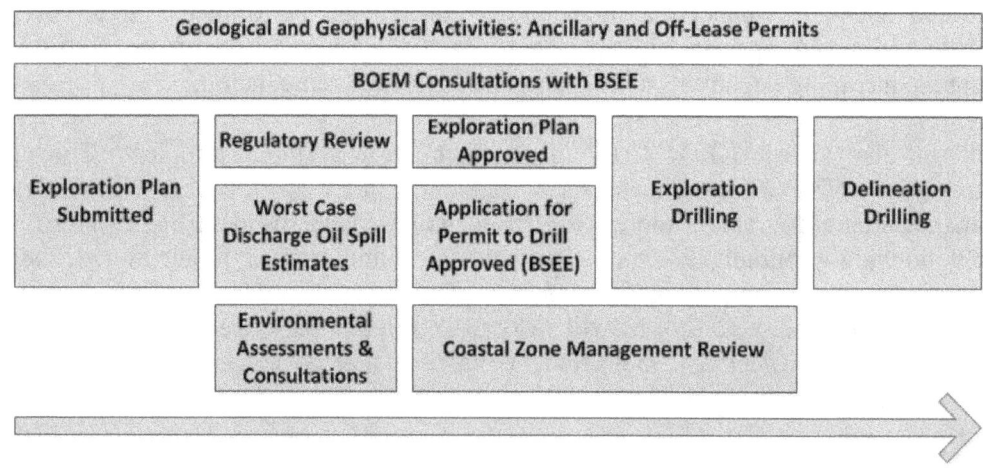

**Figure 8: Processes for Development and Approval of Development Plans**

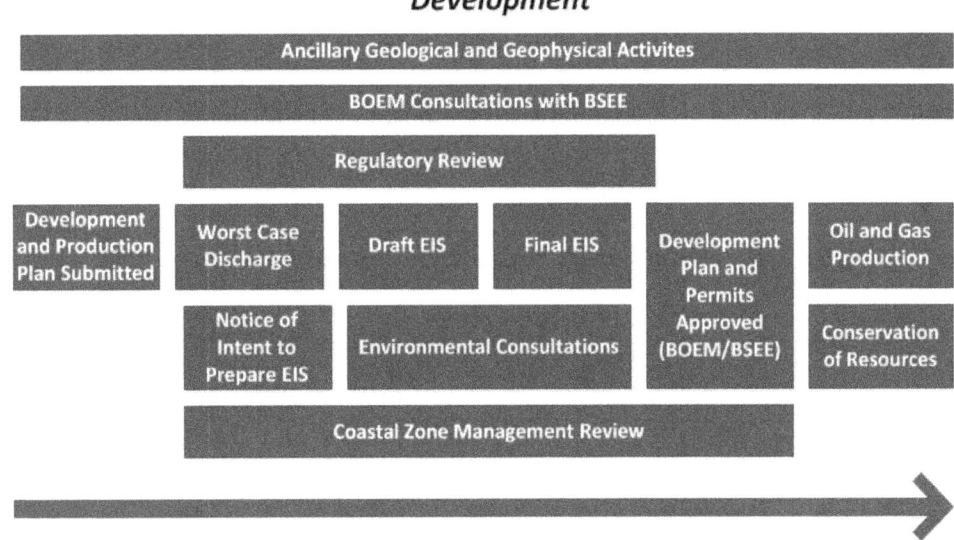

Beginning in FY 2014, BOEM will begin enhancing its TIMS information technology system in order to develop an ePlans Portal that will digitize significant elements of the plan review process, creating significant efficiencies for both industry and government that would reduce plan processing time by up to 40 percent, yield financial savings, and improve data quality.

For example, BOEM expects that ePlans will significantly reduce the number of times that plans are returned to operators, saving both government and industry staff time, and ultimately shortening the duration of the average plan review. In FY 2013, BOEM received approximately 427 plan submissions. Of the plans submitted, approximately 280 required revisions. The average time required to process and approve initial plans with no revisions was 76 days. The approximately 280 plans requiring revisions added an average of 30 days to the review process. BOEM currently returns exploration and development plans to operators an average of four times per plan – often due to errors such as incomplete fields and technical errors. With ePlans, applicants would be able to monitor the review process online and correct these types of errors in a timely manner in order to finalize their electronic transactions. BOEM expects this change to limit the number of returns to an average of one per plan, and to focus the review process on substantive corrections.

In developing the portal, BOEM will coordinate closely with BSEE, which is simultaneously developing a complementary ePermits portal. The ePlans portal is a critical component of BOEM's efforts to improve and modernize its core mission processes, and to facilitate coordination and data-sharing between BOEM, BSEE, and other state and Federal regulatory agencies. Through ePlans, information transfer can be managed effectively through a prescribed workflow for plan and NEPA reviewers, with timely decisions relayed back to the plans coordinator. System validation checks performed prior to plan submission will eliminate the need for plan coordinators and reviewers to perform these checks manually, allowing them more time to analyze non-routine plans.

***Gulf of Mexico Region:*** As of December 2013, BOEM oversees 29,089 blocks in the Gulf of Mexico Region, and of these, 5,763 are leased. There are a total of 1,318 active leases within the Western Planning Area, 4,342 active leases in the Central Planning Area, and 112 active leases in the Eastern Planning Area. Of these, there are a total of 9 active leases that are shared between the Central and Eastern Planning Areas, resulting in the grand total of 5,763 active leases within the Gulf of Mexico. A snapshot of the blocks and active leases within the Gulf of Mexico is provided below in Figure 9.

**Figure 9: Gulf of Mexico Region Blocks and Active Leases by Planning Area**

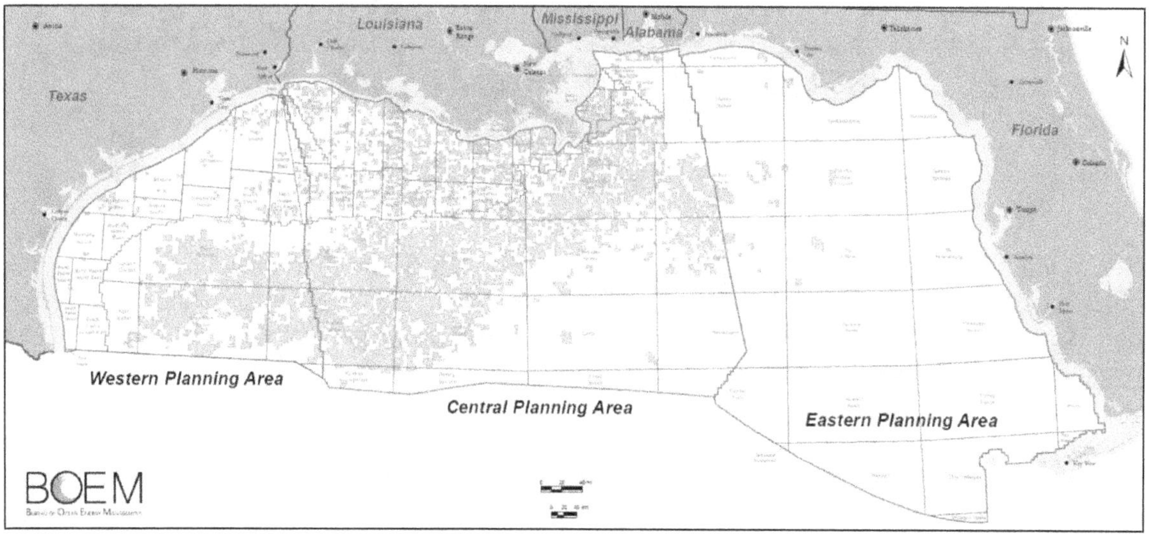

BOEM also reviews and processes all right-of-use and easement applications. Rights-of-use and easements are granted to operators to construct or maintain platforms and other installations at OCS sites on which the operator does not have an OCS lease. In FY 2013, the Gulf of Mexico Region completed 42 right-of-use and easement requests. BOEM anticipates approximately 60 requests in each of FY 2014 and FY 2015.

BOEM anticipates its 2015 workload in the Region to remain steady with respect to 2014, but this is dependent on a number of variables. For instance, proposed increases in the number of rigs in the Gulf of Mexico could also potentially increase the number of plan submittals and reviews processed by BOEM.

The following table shows all plan submittals – initial, supplemental, revised, modifications, amendments, and post approval – received from 2006 through 2013, as well as plans estimated to be received in fiscal years 2014 and 2015.

**Table 14: Plan Review Activities in the Gulf of Mexico 2008-2015**

| Calendar Year | # EPs | # DOCDs |
|---|---|---|
| 2008 | 516 | 444 |
| 2009 | 619 | 350 |
| 2010 | 408 | 431 |
| 2011 | 907* | 837* |
| 2012 | 170 | 327 |
| 2013 | 504 | 616 |
| 2014** | 554 | 678 |
| 2015** | 554 | 678 |

\* The increase in 2011 is due to heightened standards on information requirements on Exploration Plans (EP) and Development Operation Coordination Documents (DOCD) in the OCS.

\*\* The number of plans noted in 2014 and 2015 are estimated.

***Alaska Region:*** As of December 2013, the Alaska OCS contains 607 active leases encompassing approximately 3.36 million acres in the Beaufort Sea (147 leases) and Chukchi Sea (460 leases). The location of these leases offshore Alaska are shown I nthe figure below. In the coming years, BOEM anticipates receiving multiple requests to conduct ancillary activities and exploratory drilling on several of these leases, and ultimately requests for approval of development and production plans. These requests are complicated by Alaska's extreme Arctic conditions, remote location, and lack of infrastructure. The processing of these requests is often slowed by litigation, which requires extensive staff time to address.

**Figure 10: Alaska Region Active Leases**

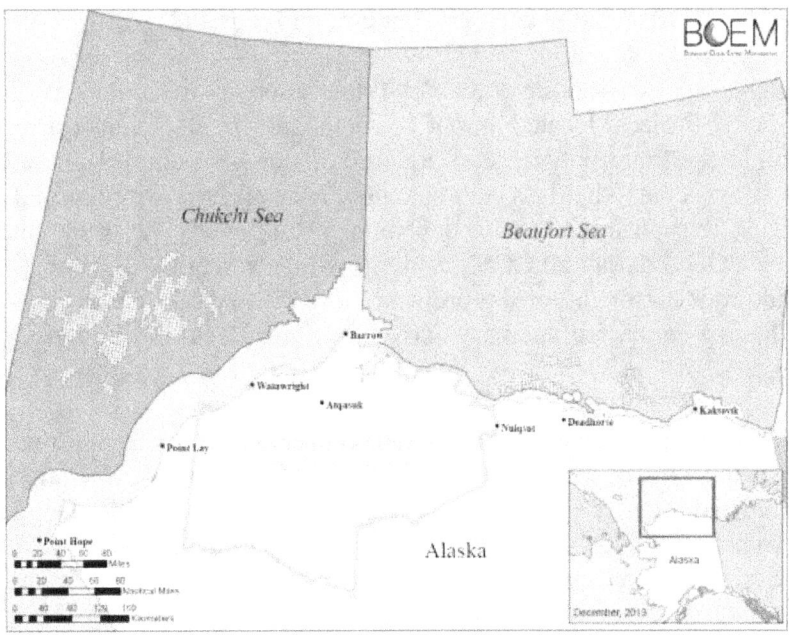

As industry interest in exploration and development on the Alaskan OCS is expected to increase in the coming years, BOEM will likely require additional staff to review and oversee offshore oil and gas drilling plans in the Beaufort and Chukchi Seas. Specifically, BOEM anticipates recruiting additional engineers with experience working in the Arctic. Experiences during the 2012 season, more fully described in the "Report to the Secretary of the Interior: Review of Shell's 2012 Alaska Offshore Oil and Gas Exploration Program," underscore the importance of rigorous planning and oversight to ensure that industry meets high standards for operating in the Arctic. The March 2013 report describes experiences such as Shell's failure to secure approval of the Arctic Containment System, inadequate oversight of key contractors, lack of compliance with air permit requirements, and problems during mobilization and demobilization. BOEM and BSEE are working to develop proposed regulations that will establish "Arctic Standards" for OCS activities, an effort that will continue through 2014 into 2015.

In 2011, BOEM conditionally approved exploration plans from Shell Offshore, Inc. and Shell Gulf of Mexico, Inc. for multiple year and multiple well activities in the Beaufort and Chukchi Seas. Following grounding of the *Kulluk* in late 2012, Shell called a "pause" to exploration drilling activities in 2013 to resolve issues associated with its 2012 exploration program. In November 2013, Shell submitted a revised exploration plan for its Chukchi Sea leases. Recently, Shell announced that it would not conduct exploratory drilling in 2014, due to the legal uncertainty created by Ninth Circuit Court of Appeals decision remanding the NEPA analysis supporting Chukchi Sea Lease Sale 193 (from which Shell's leases were issued) to the district court.

A second multiple year and multiple well plan in the Chukchi Sea was received from ConocoPhillips, Inc. in March 2012; however, BOEM required additional information before the plan could be deemed submitted. In April 2013, ConocoPhillips announced it was putting its 2014 Alaska Chukchi Sea exploration drilling plans on hold. This announcement followed the Department's previously mentioned publication " Report to the Secretary of the Interior: Review of Shell's 2012 Alaska Offshore Oil and Gas Exploration Program."

Meanwhile, BOEM is also working with BP Exploration as the company pursues plans to develop the Liberty Project, located in OCS waters north of Prudhoe Bay. The Liberty development will be the first solely Federal offshore oil and gas complex in the U.S. Arctic, and its development is expected to help lay the foundations for all future offshore oil and gas activity in the U.S. Arctic. Responsible and safe development of Liberty, as wellas the same rigorous oversight used by BOEM during all OCS planning, will be essential. BP is required to submit a development and production plan for the project before the end of calendar year 2014 and is on track to do so, having conducted ancillary activities in the Beaufort Sea during the winter and summer of 2013 and 2014.

Review of exploration and development and production plans requires additional environmental consultation with the U.S. Fish and Wildlife Service (FWS) and the National Oceanic and Atmospheric Administration (NOAA) to ensure compliance with the Endangered Species Act and Marine Mammal Protection Act, as well as other laws protecting the environment. BOEM also consults with NOAA on marine mammals and essential fish habitat, and with the State Historic Preservation Offices on archaeology and historic preservation requirements. In accordance with treaty obligations, the BOEM initiates and engages in government-to-government consultations with federally recognized tribes and Alaska Native Claims Settlement Act Corporations in planning activities that may have a substantial direct effect on native communities.

***Pacific Region:*** While the current Five Year Program does not include lease sales in the Pacific Region, BOEM continues to oversee activity on 43 existing leases from previous sales. Proposed activities on these active leases periodically require an update or revision to development and production plans. Figure 11 below shows the location of these leases off the coast of Southern California

**Figure 11: Pacific Region Active Leases**

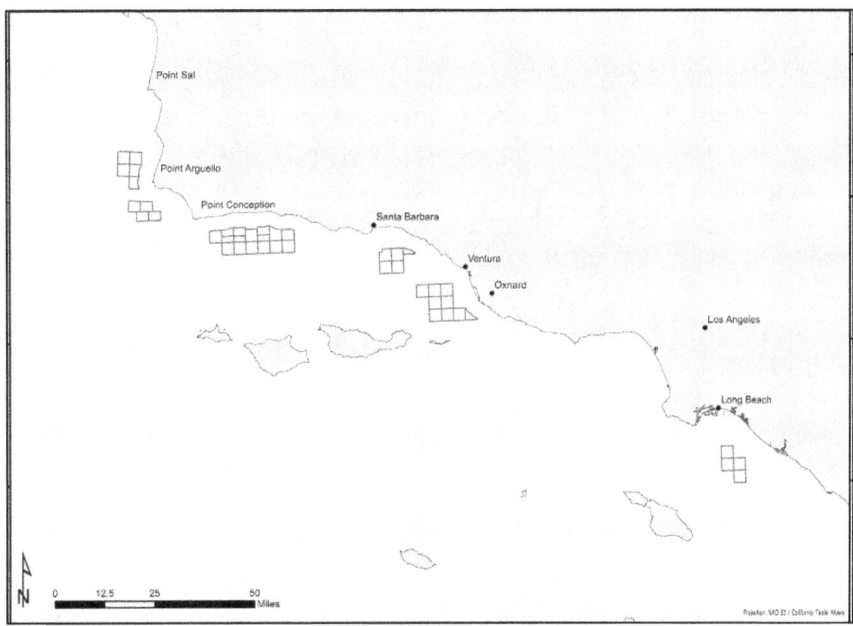

During FY 2013, BOEM reviewed three such updates, and expects three more in each of FY 2014 and FY 2015. Federal Platform Irene, offshore north of Point Arguello, has, in the past, been proposed for use in development of state reserves in the Tranquillon Ridge field. If the California State Lands Commission provides the opportunity for a state lease and the operator of the adjacent Federal lease proposes this development from Platform Irene, BOEM will require review and revision to the existing Federal development and production plan.

> ➢ **Oil Spill Financial Responsibility Program**

The financial responsibilities associated with the development of offshore resources are enormous. Just as BOEM must protect the American taxpayer from entities that fail to meet their lease, grant, or permit obligations, the Bureau must also ensure that these same entities have the financial resources to pay for cleanup and damages that could be caused by oil discharges from their offshore facilities. Under the Oil Pollution Act, liability for damages from offshore facility spills is capped at $75 million, unless it can be shown that the responsible party was guilty of willful miscounduct, gross negligence, failed to report the incident or cooperate with removal activities, or violated a federal safety regulation, in which case there is no limit on damages. On February 24, 2014, BOEM published a proposed rule that would increase this cap to over $130 million, based on adjustments for inflation. BOEM performs a through review and oversight of industry oil spill financial responsibility filings, which are required before any drilling activities are approved. BOEM uses the information to (1) ensure Oil Pollution Act compliance by offshore lessees and owners and operators of covered facilities, (2) establish eligibility of designated applicants for oil spill financial responsibility certification, and (3) establish reference and contact information for potentially responsible parties, their designated agents and guarantors. The program currently oversees approximately 160 companies covering 7,500 facilities with financial coverage in excess of $11 billion.

> ## Worst Case Discharge

BOEM defines a worst case discharge for exploratory and development drilling operations as the daily rate of an uncontrolled flow of oil and gas from all producible reservoirs through the open wellbore. The package of reservoirs exposed to an open borehole with the greatest discharge potential is considered the worst case discharge scenario. Current regulations require operators and lessees to submit worst case discharge calculated volumes and associated data as part of every exploration plan and development plan.

Each Region is responsible for worst case discharge verifications and decision documentation associated with plans under their jurisdictions. BOEM geoscientists and engineers independently verify the validity of the volume calculations, assumptions, and analogs used by the operator for the worst case discharge. BOEM's worst case discharge model outputs are also used by BSEE in reviewing oil spill response plans and making Application for Permit to Drill decisions.

*Gulf of Mexico Region:* BOEM made determinations on 109 worst case discharge verifications in FY 2013. In FY 2014 and FY 2015, BOEM does not anticipate a decrease in worst case discharge analyses, though the workload will depend on the level of drilling activity in deepwater. BOEM continues to develop trend parameters for deepwater exploration and development drilling for critical reservoir and fluid properties for the worst case discharge analysis in order to enhance the efficiency of the process while maintaining the regulatory oversight needed to ensure an adequate response to an uncontrolled blowout. BOEM is also participating in the Society of Petroleum Engineers Worst Case Discharge Summit in New Orleans, March 16-18, 2014. The purpose of the Worst Case Discharge Summit is to provide best-practice guidelines for calculating the volume of an uncontrolled wellbore flow event, and to discuss and resolve complex issues encountered in various worst-case scenarios.

*Alaska Region:* In FY 2013, BOEM consulted with three different companies on their first Alaska worst case discharge estimates. In FY 2014, BOEM anticipates formal submission of these estimates. The worst case discharge estimates have heightened importance in Alaska because there are no readily available oil spill response capabilities for the Arctic marine environment that operators can access and allow sharing of costs. For example, in the Gulf of Mexico, operators can obtain a membership in an oil spill response organization where the members can share the cost of the response capability needed to clean-up an estimated worst case discharge for their wells. Currently in Alaska, each operator must provide their own response capability to cover an estimated worst case discharge volume. Operators request numerous meetings with BOEM staff to clarify the various input parameters and assumptions in reservoir flow simulation software models that provide the worst case discharge estimates in their attempt to produce a valid estimate. Another first-time worst case discharge project for the Alaska staff will be evaluating the worst case discharge submittal for the proposed Liberty field development.

*Pacific Region*:  In FY 2013, the Region completed two worst case discharge verifications. Because there is no new leasing, the Region's worst case discharge analyses are for mature fields only. The projected workload for worst case discharge reviews for FY 2014 and 2015 is anticipated to be between three to four annually.

> **G&G Regulatory Reviews**

Geological and geophysical (G&G) reviews are performed to evaluate drilling hazards posed by surface and subsurface geologic conditions and man-made obstructions (30 CFR 550.201-207). In addition, geophysical reviews are performed to evaluate shallow hazards (seafloor and near seafloor) on operators' applications for pipeline rights-of-way and associated permits (30 CFR 250.1007 (5)). These reviews include evaluation and verification of operator's interpretations, identification and assessment of potential geohazards in the area affected by exploratory and development drilling, installation of structures, laying pipelines, and other ancillary activities related to the plans. Based on G&G surveys from operators, geoscientists identify and evaluate potential risk of shallow faulting, shallow gas zone, shallow water flows, abnormal pressure zones, lost circulation zones, and other natural and manmade hazards. In addition, geoscientists evaluate the potential risk of encountering hydrogen sulfide ($H_2S$), a toxic gas. The G&G reviews provide a detailed evaluation of operators' geohazards analyses and shallow hazards assessment and determine mitigations to be applied to plan and permit approvals.

Geoscientists conduct G&G evaluations that include broaching analyses that support BSEE reviews and approvals of operators' APDs for wells. The integrity of the well design is evaluated by BSEE, and if a determination is made that the well may fail at a certain casing point, a broaching analysis is conducted by geoscientists. The broaching analysis evaluates subsurface stratigraphic and structural conditions to determine if escaping hydrocarbons from a failed casing shoe will be trapped in the formations or potentially reach the seafloor at some point in time.

*Gulf of Mexico Region:*  In FY 2013, BOEM conducted 340 geological and 432 geophysical reviews in support of plans, renewable energy site characterization, and BSEE APD and pipeline responsibilities. Moving forward, increasingly complex analyses will be required for geohazard reviews due to higher resolution data collected for complex projects, especially those occurring in deepwater, and the additional workload of broaching analysis in support of the BSEE well integrity analysis. In FY 2013, broaching analyses were completed on 27 proposed wells, and a comparable number of wells will be reviewed for well integrity in both fiscal years 2013 and 2014.

***Alaska Region*:**  In FY 2013, there was a hiatus in exploration drilling, but the collection of shallow hazard data for future exploration and development continued, and is expected to do so in FY 2014 as well.  An increase in drilling is probable in FY 2015 based on discussions with companies holding leases that are approaching the lease term time limits.

## MAPPING AND BOUNDARY

The Secretary of the Interior is charged by law with the administration of offshore submerged lands on the OCS for offshore energy and minerals leasing purposes.  Various court decisions, treaties, legislation, policies, and procedures guide the boundary making process on the OCS. The offshore submerged lands of the OCS are subdivided into parcels referred to as OCS blocks. No submerged lands may be offered for leases that are not owned by the Federal Government, and no submerged federally-owned lands may be offered for lease or sale by either a foreign country or a U.S. Coastal State.  For these reasons, accurate offshore lease boundary lines are a foundational requirement for all BOEM offshore leasing activities.  Through its mapping and boundary functions, both in the headquarters and the regions, BOEM is responsible for producing and maintaining the official marine cadastre for the Federal OCS areas of the United States.

The current focus of this work is to generate the blocks and boundary lines necessary to support leasing for renewable energy purposes in the offshore areas of Hawaii.  Customized Geographic Information Systems (GIS) tools are being used for this effort, which will continue through 2015.  A joint request to the U.S. Supreme Court from BOEM and California to fix (immobilize) the Submerged Lands Act (SLA) boundary for that state is in the final stage of review by the Department of Justice.  After the review, the decree will be placed on the Supreme Court docket. Fixing the SLA boundary will provide certainty to lessors, regulators, lessees, and operators of Federal and state mineral and renewable energy leases and will prevent future litigation concerning the submerged lands rights of both parties.  The SLA boundary has already been fixed for the north coast of Alaska and all of the Gulf of Mexico states except for Florida. Oregon and Washington are interested in fixing their SLA boundaries, as are several Atlantic Coast States.  Should the Supreme Court approve fixing of the California SLA boundary, subsequent mapping requests will be easier and hopefully faster to complete.  BOEM is working with all interested coastal states to reach agreement on the location of their respective SLA boundary in anticipation of future efforts to fix other SLA boundaries.

## MARINE CADASTRE

The MarineCadastre.gov project is a web-based integrated marine information system that provides an authoritative source of ocean information, including offshore boundaries, infrastructure, ocean uses, habitat distribution data, energy potential, and other data sets important to large regional ocean planning efforts, as well as project-specific planning. Data is provided as immediate viewable map data, downloadable GIS formatted data, and as map services. Most data are available directly from the authoritative source, or are updated regularly from the source(s). MarineCadastre.gov was created to comply with Section 388 of the Energy Policy Act of 2005, which mandated a comprehensive digital mapping initiative for decision-making on the OCS, and is also providing the geospatial framework needed for the broader ocean planning initiative called for in the National Ocean Policy. MarineCadastre.gov has three primary focus areas: web map viewers and ocean planning tools; spatial data registry; and technical support and regional capacity building.

> *MarineCadastre.gov* products were designed for use by Federal regulatory agencies, regional marine planners, state intergovernmental task forces, and the offshore wind energy industry.

In addition to the data sets provided by other authoritative data providers – such as NOAA, FWS, U.S. Geological Survey, U.S. Coast Guard, U.S. Navy, and others – the MarineCadastre.gov includes a variety of BOEM/BSEE data sets. Users inside and outside of BOEM have access to the most up to date versions of lease maps, protractions, lease blocks, boundaries, pipelines, wells, and other BOEM/BSEE generated GIS data important to BOEM's stakeholders for marine planning and energy development planning purposes. The data and services provided through the MarineCadastre.gov project are used by a number of regional ocean portal projects, fulfilling BOEM's vision for the project to be the first place to find authoritative coastal and marine data.

BOEM's efforts on the MarineCadastre.gov have been recognized by the Center for Environmental Innovation and Leadership (CEIL) for "Success through Collaboration" with the NOAA's Coastal Services Center. The CEIL Awards recognize military and Federal teams and programs that have demonstrated exemplary performance in integrating environmental stewardship into day-to-day activities and turned sustainability ideas into reality. Awards highlight excellence in developing and implementing innovative environmental programs to improve environmental quality, reduce greenhouse gas emissions, or increase use of renewable energy and bio-preferred products.

MarineCadastre.gov is constantly evolving and growing to include relevant issue-driven data and tools. Specialized maps in the "Gallery Page" of the project are available. Ocean planners can create custom data viewers by combining authoritative data from the Marine Cadastre Data Registry with more locally relevant web map services. BOEM is currently focusing on strengthening biodiversity and ocean use data by helping provide access to data from authoritative sources, educating the users about the data and its uses, and building decision support tools to support coastal and marine planning.

## ECONOMIC EVALUATION

A critical component of BOEM's mission is to ensure the receipt of fair market value for offshore natural resources. To accomplish this, BOEM employs a team of interdisciplinary experts that provide economic analyses for the Department of the Interior, other Federal agencies, and Congress. To ensure fair market value, BOEM develops various resource-economic evaluation approaches and bid adequacy guidelines, determines economic inputs for tract evaluation, and coordinates reviews of appeals of bid rejection. BOEM's economic analysis expertise is often called upon to analyze and implement regulatory and legislative actions affecting OCS leasing, exploration, development, and production activities which generate significant supplies of domestic oil and gas and which result in the receipt of billions of dollars each year to the U.S. Treasury. BOEM also undertakes studies, as needed, to address specific policies and compilations of data required to analyze overall OCS program responsibilities and initiatives. BOEM's economic functions support all programmatic activities, conventional oil and gas, renewable energy, and mineral leasing.

> ## Fair Market Value

BOEM's economic experts develop, evaluate, and identify models, policies and parameters designed to ensure receipt of fair market value for the rights to explore and produce offshore energy and mineral resources.

> ## Bid Evaluation

*Bid Evaluation*
The Bureau uses a two-phase post-sale bid evaluation process to meet the fair market value requirement. The Bureau reviews all high bids received and evaluates all blocks using either tract-specific bidding factors or detailed tract-specific analytical factors to ensure that fair market value is received for each OCS lease issued. This bid adequacy process relies on both evidence of market competition and in-house estimates of tract value.

BOEM conducts analyses to support development of regulations and evaluation of policies for lease terms, conditions, and bidding systems for individual oil and gas lease sales, the Five Year Program, the Renewable Energy Program, and for the use of sites for construction of liquefied natural gas ports upon request of the U.S. Coast Guard. Under its bid adequacy procedures, the Bureau reviews all high bids received and evaluates all blocks using either tract-specific bidding factors or detailed tract-specific analytic factors to ensure that fair market value is received for each OCS lease issued. The bid adequacy process relies on both evidence of market competition and in-house estimates of tract value. If a bid is rejected and a company appeals the rejection, the staff reviews the appeal and makes a recommendation to the Director regarding the appeal.

In addition to the fiscal terms and bid adequacy process, the Bureau establishes terms and conditions to assure diligent development of leases and environmentally safe and clean operations.

➢ **Receipt Estimates**

BOEM's economic experts review and design policies and methods for forecasting receipts from the offshore energy programs, including the estimation of the manner and rate at which reserves and resources of oil and gas are discovered and produced. Through the economics function, BOEM generates the receipt estimates used to project revenue and offsetting collections amounts identified in the annual President's budget. These estimates also provide a means for forecasting the comparative share of receipts from offshore oil and gas that will be owed to the states under various revenue sharing programs, assist in assessing alternative operator diligence requirements, and contribute to policies for setting timely and efficient requirements for drilling initial wells and decommissioning existing wells and structures.

➢ **Economic Modeling for Policy and Decision-Making**

BOEM's efforts contribute significantly to the development of national energy strategies. Bureau experts develop and maintain economic and statistical models and databases that are the basis for sale design, Five Year Program formulation, resource evaluation, post-sale and operational activities, rulemaking, revenue sharing, and royalty relief programs. The economic assumptions and scenarios BOEM generates are used in post-sale tract evaluations, national resource assessment studies, and in applications submitted for royalty relief. Finally, BOEM provides economic analyses and fiscal forecasts for energy leasing policies, legal and legislative alternatives, and national energy strategies.

## RESOURCE EVALUATION

Before any of the aforementioned economic analysis can occur, BOEM must first identify what resources are available, where they are located, and whether they might be technically recoverable. Through its resource evaluation function, BOEM conducts technical analyses to identify areas of the OCS that are the most promising for energy and mineral development (including methane hydrates). To accomplish this, BOEM:

- Acquires G&G data/information through the regulation of pre-lease exploration of the OCS;

- Delineates and develops estimates of the quantities of undiscovered technically and economically recoverable resources that may exist and the volume of reserves discovered and likely to be produced;

- Tracks the volume of discovered reserves, produced reserves and remaining reserves by field;

- Forecasts future industry activity levels and develops scenarios for the leasing program; and

- Determines the adequacy of high bids received for individual tracts offered for lease to ensure the Nation receives fair market value for the tracts.

BOEM's evaluation of geological, engineering, and geophysical data and information provides the inputs to the economic and statistical analyses that inform leasing policies and program decisions, such as the design of financial terms for lease sales. Program analyses assist in exploration and development plan decisions and help reduce the risk of safety and environmental concerns in offshore development decision-making.

➢ **Resource Assessment**

As one of the first steps in the leasing process, BOEM must identify geologic plays, areas on the OCS that offer the highest potential for the occurrence of oil and gas development and production. Following the identification of hydrocarbon plays, BOEM assesses the play's hydrocarbon potential and its economic viability with the help of complex computer models and methodologies. The assessment process incorporates specific geologic, petroleum engineering, and economic data and information. In addition to the estimation of undiscovered hydrocarbon resources, these studies help identify environmental and operational constraints and assist in making leasing decisions. Comparing the data for acreage and resources offered illustrates that BOEM offers access to geologic areas on the OCS that have the highest potential for development of oil and gas. BOEM also estimates the amounts of oil and gas likely to be discovered and produced as a result of leasing, and generates potential scenarios of future industrial activities associated with exploration, development, and production. BOEM measures both the resources and acres offered annually compared to what was planned for the year and analyzes the results to inform the Five Year Program and sale decisions. Resource estimates support critical analyses of potential impacts of policy options, legislative proposals, NEPA analyses, and industry activities affecting OCS oil and gas activities — both current and future.

The scale of the assessment activities range from large (regional or OCS-wide) to sale-specific, such as individual prospects and lease tracts. In the early stages of this process, the focus is on regional areas, but as more data and information are acquired, the focus shifts to lease sales and prospect-specific areas to be offered for lease, or that are related to a specific issue, (i.e., moratoria, marine sanctuaries, quantitative analysis of legislative proposals). Once a sale area has been identified, BOEM's mapping and boundary experts produce the more detailed mapping and analyses needed to estimate the resource potential of individual prospects within that area. These prospect-specific data, maps, and analyses are also used to determine parameters for post-sale bid analyses in support of fair market value evaluations.

The *2011 Assessment of Undiscovered Technically Recoverable Oil and Gas Resources of the Nation's Outer Continental Shelf* was developed to support the 2012-2017 Five Year Program. This type of assessment lays the groundwork to support activities for the next Five Year Program, and upcoming assessments will support the development of the 2017-2022 Five Year Plan. Assessment activities associated with the Five Year Program will continue to examine specific plan related issues, such as individual sales.

*Gulf of Mexico Region*: During FY 2014 and FY 2015, BOEM will continue to enhance and refine the analysis provided to support the *2011 Assessment of Undiscovered Technically Recoverable Oil and Gas Resources of the Nation's Outer Continental Shelf*. This assessment typically corresponds with the development of a new Five Year Program and is expected to be completed within the third or fourth quarter of FY 2015. Additionally, BOEM will continue work in FY 2014 to update the resource inventory for Atlantic planning areas. These efforts will provide valuable data that will be used to make informed decisions regarding the next Five Year Program, potential impacts of policy options, legislative proposals, Environmental Impact Statements, and industry activities affecting OCS oil and gas activities both current and future.

*Alaska Region:* In FY 2015, BOEM plans to reassess the oil and gas potential for both the Chukchi and Beaufort Seas in response to expected new well drilling in these sparsely drilled regions, as well as the Cook Inlet, where new seismic surveys are planned. This data will be critical for fair market value determinations for BOEM sales currently scheduled in 2016 and 2017 and for an updated national assessment for the upcoming 2017-2022 Five Year Program. BOEM's Alaska Region is responsible for all reservoir and field analyses for BOEM and BSEE in Alaska, and also all the shallow hazard reviews for exploration and development plans and subsequent applications for permit to drill.

➤ **Fair Market Value Determination**

Ensuring the receipt of fair market value on the Outer Continental Shelf is mandated by the OCS Lands Act and is one of BOEM's critical responsibilities. Regional offices, with headquarters coordination and oversight, perform the functions necessary to thoroughly assess the oil and gas potential and fair market value of OCS tracts offered for lease. Only tracts located within leasing areas identified in the Five Year Program are available for lease. The bid review process incorporates G&G data along with reserve, resource, engineering, and economic information, which is provided by the BOEM economic subject matter experts, into a sophisticated discounted cash flow computer model that estimates economic value of the corresponding tract. The goal of that model is to achieve independent estimates of fair market value on tracts receiving bids.

> Since 1984, *bid adequacy* determinations have resulted in an average rejection rate of bids of approximately 3.8 percent. Bid adequacy procedures have consistently resulted in higher returns in subsequent sales for tracts that have had bids rejected on fair market value grounds in previous sales. From 1984 through 2013, BOEM has rejected total high bids of approximately $630 million. Subsequently, the same blocks were re-offered and drew high bids of $1.8 billion, for a total net gain of approximately $1.2 billion.

*Gulf of Mexico Region:* Under the current Five Year Program, three OCS oil and gas lease sales are scheduled for FY 2014, as indicated earlier in Table 13. The sales include: Eastern Gulf of Mexico Sale 225 and Central Gulf of Mexico Sale 231 (to be held concurrently in March 2014), and Western Gulf of Mexico Sale 238 (scheduled to occur in the summer of 2014). Bids received during these lease sales will undergo rigorous fair market value determinations.

*Alaska Region:* Although no lease sales are planned in the Alaska Region until 2016, the Region still conducts valuable analyses for other Federal agencies. For instance, BOEM continues to provide the Bureau of Land Management (BLM) with fair market value analyses on National Petroleum Reserve–Alaska lease sales. It is estimated that this level of activity will continue since single sales in the National Petroleum Reserve–Alaska are scheduled in both 2014 and 2015. To improve efficiency in these efforts and mitigate potential staffing shortages, BOEM is evaluating sophisticated software options to replace existing, cash flow modeling programs.

➢ **Reserves Inventory Program**

The OCS Lands Act requires the Department to "conduct a continuing investigation…for the purpose of determining the availability of all oil and gas produced or located on the Outer Continental Shelf." In order to meet this requirement, BOEM is required to develop independent estimates of economically recoverable amounts of oil and gas contained within discovered fields by conducting field reserve studies. The reserve estimates are revised periodically to reflect new information obtained from development and production activities.

Reserve studies are critical inputs to resource assessments, the review and approval of royalty relief applications, as analogs for bid adequacy determinations, and in the review of industry plans and requests. The geologic and engineering information also support other program activities within the Department and cooperative efforts with the Department of Energy and its Energy Information Administration.

*Gulf of Mexico Region*: At the Regional level, reserves inventory personnel review conservation information document submissions. Conservation information documents are required to ensure operators exploit all economic reservoir accumulations discovered rather than producing only the most prolific zones and bypassing marginally economic zones. The review and analysis of company-submitted conservation information documents allows for the maximum ultimate recovery and full development of economic reserves and resources, while ensuring fair monetary compensation for the Federal Government. Additionally, BOEM anticipates the evaluation of approximately 16 requests in FY 2015 associated with well abandonment and bypassed zones to ensure that operators are following their conservation information document commitments.

During FY 2014, BOEM anticipates issuing a number of reports summarizing oil and gas reserves and production from Gulf of Mexico discovered fields. The calendar year 2010 and 2011 reports on "Estimated Oil and Gas Reserves Gulf of Mexico OCS Region" will be published on the BOEM website in FY 2014. As required in the Energy Policy Act of 2005, the Region will provide support to headquarters in generating the *4th Biennial Report to Congress: Estimates of Natural Gas and Oil Reserves, Reserves Growth, and Undiscovered Resources in Federal and State Waters off the Coasts of Texas, Louisiana, Mississippi, and Alabama.* Oil and gas resources located off the coasts of Texas, Louisiana, Mississippi and Alabama are important to the future domestic energy supply of the United States. These areas are available for leasing through various state and Federal leasing programs.

*Alaska Region:* BOEM continues to support BSEE in the oversight of production allocation issues for the Northstar field unit which produces oil from both State of Alaska and OCS leases.

*Pacific Region*: During FY 2013, BOEM generated its annual Field Reservoir and Reserve Estimate report, breaking down the Pacific Region's reserves and known resources by field and productive zone. Work on this annual report begins once production data is submitted by companies, which is typically received by BOEM in the late spring or early summer. BOEM then must verify the data and perform a variety of analyses, which typically takes months to complete. The Field Reservoir and Reserve report provides a brief update on reserves and production between releases of the more comprehensive Estimated Oil and Gas Reserves report. BOEM anticipates publishing an annual Field Reservoir and Reserve Estimate report during FY 2014 and also FY 2015.

## ➤ Regulation of Prelease Exploration

Through regulation, BOEM works to ensure that prelease exploration, prospecting, and scientific research operations in Federal waters do not interfere with each other, with lease operations, or with other permitted uses of the area. Permits to acquire prelease geological and geophysical data identify specific parameters for each activity, including the area of interest, the timing of acquisition, the use of approved equipment and methods, and required environmental compliance measures. For each approved application, the operator receives a signed copy of the permit that outlines policies regarding reporting, submission, inspection and selection of data, reimbursement, disclosure of information, possible sharing of data with affected states, and policies regarding permit modifications. Adherence to these regulations ensures that exploration and research activities will be conducted in a safe and environmentally sound manner.

*Gulf of Mexico Region*: BOEM will continue to issue permits for both oil and gas exploration and marine minerals prospecting activities. Annual permitting activity in the Region has been relatively steady over the last several years. During FY 2015, the BOEM anticipates evaluating and issuing approximately 50 permits, as well as various permit modifications, with the majority of the permits issued for deep penetration seismic surveys. The challenge is to balance the increased need for coordination with NEPA and other environmental reviews while providing the permittee with timely access to permits to meet their business operation needs.

*Alaska Region:* BOEM will continue to issue permits for both oil and gas exploration and marine minerals prospecting activities (e.g. gold). Permit activity is expected to remain at two to six permits submitted per year, primarily seismic surveys for off-lease exploration. In addition to ensuring that all permittees adhere to statutory requirements (including the Marine Mammal Protection Act and the Endangered Species Act), BOEM also coordinates with other Federal agency efforts, community involvement and government-to-government consultations (e.g., tribal consultations and Alaska Native Claims Settlement Act Corporations). Because of the outreach required, these efforts involve a higher level of personnel resources and commitment to manage these permits. BOEM's workload in FY 2014 and 2015 will likely depend on the level of activity in the Region, for instance scheduled OCS lease sales, particularly in the Cook Inlet where the last successful OCS sale was held in 1997, or if a major discovery is made in the Arctic OCS.

### ➢ G&G Data Acquisition and Analysis

Critical to identifying potential resources on the OCS is the acquisition and analysis of geological and geophysical (G&G) data. This enables BOEM to identify areas favorable for the accumulation of hydrocarbons and develop estimates of resource volumes and economic values of these accumulations. These estimates are used to focus OCS leasing on areas of high potential, as well as to help assure fair market value in lease sale bid evaluations.

The majority of BOEM business processes where oil and gas resources are assessed – such as the reserve inventory program, fair market value analysis, and resource assessment – are based on the analysis of large volumes of G&G data. The primary source of the G&G data BOEM uses is physically acquired by the oil and gas industry, which conducts exploration, development, and production activities on OCS lands. As a condition of the permit that BOEM issues prior to each industry activity (such as seismic data acquisition), companies are required to provide a copy of the G&G data to BOEM upon request after completion of data acquisition. BOEM uses these data internally, while maintaining them in a proprietary term that generally ranges from 2 to 25 years. The extensive amount of data and information acquired is used by BOEM and BSEE geologists, geophysicists, and petroleum engineers to perform a variety of analyses leading to resource estimates, reserve inventories, and determining fair market value of the leased tracts.

*Atlantic OCS:* In FY 2014 BOEM will begin to acquire and maintain G&G data within the Mid- and South Atlantic. A total of 28 pending permits from eight companies have been submitted as of January 2014. Facilitating resource evaluation in the Mid- and South Atlantic planning areas is a high priority for BOEM and the Administration, and the strategy for future efforts in those areas was laid out in the Five Year Program, as approved by the Secretary in August 2012. The region-specific strategy laid out in the Five Year Program was designed to support future decision-making regarding whether potential offshore oil and gas lease sales in the Mid- and South Atlantic planning areas would be appropriate, and if so, where future lease sales should be focused.

BOEM's strategy will support development of modern, robust scientific information about the scope and location of potential oil and gas resources in the Mid- and South Atlantic and to facilitate resolution of significant potential conflicts between oil and gas activity and other important OCS uses in these areas, including military, fishing, and vessel traffic uses as well as environmental and infrastructure concerns. Collection, acquisition and analysis of this data is an important component of this overall effort.

*Gulf of Mexico Region*: Both BOEM and industry are expanding their use of three-dimensional technology to study and evaluate the complex geologic picture of the Gulf of Mexico OCS. The data provided by this technology is used by decision-makers to inform policies regarding offshore resource development in the Gulf of Mexico.

Because it oversees such a large number of active leases, the Gulf of Mexico Region acquires, analyzes and manages a vast collection of G&G data. BOEM currently manages approximately 2,121 three-dimensional surveys, 506 two-dimensional surveys, and other critical data encompassing a total volume of 117 terabytes. Data volumes grow at a rate of approximately 15 terabytes per year. To effectively manage the growing volumes, BOEM actively invests in data management solutions (servers, disk space, Hierarchical Storage Management, database development) needed to effectively store, archive, manage, and deliver geophysical data to BOEM and BSEE users, as well as other stakeholders (e.g., other Federal agencies and the public).

*Alaska Region:* BOEM continues to acquire and manage critical data needed to support mission functions, such as the development of lease sale environmental impact statement scenarios, Five Year Program scenarios, and lease sale fair market value determinations. If exploration drilling increases in the Arctic, more staff time will be devoted to managing and protecting the increasing amounts of data and information critical for detailed analyses needed by both BOEM and BSEE. It is expected that this workload will remain fairly constant in 2014, but could increase in 2015 due to anticipated Arctic drilling activities and pre-lease G&G permitted activities in preparation for lease sales scheduled in 2016 and 2017.

## MARINE MINERALS PROGRAM

BOEM is responsible for the policy and guidance for the development of all OCS minerals other than oil, gas, and sulphur under Section 8(k) of the OCS Lands Act and is the sole responsible steward of OCS sand, gravel and shell resources critical for the long-term success and cost-effectiveness of many shore protection, beach nourishment, and wetlands restoration projects along the Gulf and Atlantic coasts. The OCS Lands Act, as amended, authorizes BOEM to convey, on a noncompetitive basis, the rights to OCS sediment resources to Federal, state, and local entities for shore protection, beach or wetlands restoration projects, or for use in construction projects funded or authorized by the Federal Government. In addition to being a statutory responsibility, activities of the Marine Minerals Program also reflect a strategic investment in advance planning, sand resource evaluation, stakeholder coordination and environmental assessment and study so that, when they are needed, OCS sand resources can be made available in a responsible way.

The Marine Minerals Program provides the Bureau with the capability to provide sand and gravel resources to protect and improve coastal resources and the environment locally, regionally and nationally. To date, BOEM (and its predecessor the Minerals Mangement Service) has conveyed the rights to more than 77 million cubic yards of OCS sediment in 42 projects covering six states and 229 miles of coastline. In FY 2012, BOEM issued three noncompetitive agreements to provide more than 11 million cubic yards of OCS sand. During FY 2013, demand for these resources increased dramatically due to recovery and restoration efforts related to Hurricane Sandy. In FY 2013, BOEM negotiated eight noncompetitive agreements to provide more than 6.1 million cubic yards of OCS sand for coastal restoration/wetlands protection projects along the Atlantic and Gulf of Mexico. As these projects continue into FY 2014, BOEM anticipates completing nine agreements conveying approximately 30 million cubic yards of OCS sand, the largest amount of OCS sand conveyed in one year.

BOEM is responsible for managing the use of mineral resources and ensuring that the

### *Coastal Impacts of Storms and Erosion*

As Hurricane Sandy illustrated (shown in the images below), natural and developed coasts are frequently subject to major storm damage and severe erosion. OCS sand resources are often needed under urgent circumstances to restore damaged shorelines and wetlands to pre-storm condition, or are needed more strategically to protect coastal areas in advance of a storm, or to re-establish important biological habitat and ecological function. In some regions, like the Gulf of Mexico, sufficient volume of sand resources for use in the long-term ecosystem scale restoration of barrier islands and wetlands is only available on the OCS. Along Atlantic and Gulf Coasts, BOEM anticipates the demand for, and importance of, OCS sand resources will continue to rise because of climate-related changes in storm activity and accelerating sea level rise, as well as an increasing number of environmental and resource conflicts in state waters.

**NASA Flight Facility at Wallops Island, Virginia**

conveyance of OCS sand resources does not result in adverse environmental impacts on the marine, coastal, or human environment. Each negotiated lease requires a NEPA analysis, including endangered species and essential fish habitat consultations with the National Marine Fisheries Service (NMFS) and the FWS, as well as coastal consistency and archaeological resources reviews. BOEM plans to continue to initiate studies to provide information to evaluate the effects of specific proposed dredging operations, as required under current environmental laws, and design mitigation measures that are incorporated, as appropriate, in lease requirements and stipulations for the dredging of OCS sands.

Many of the completed projects used sand from OCS borrow areas that were identified by the highly successful state cooperative offshore sand agreements that were in place from the mid-1990s to 2005. Sand deposits previously identified and evaluated by the program have been used for 17 beach nourishment projects in Maryland, Virginia, Louisiana, and Florida. Sand sources identified through the cooperative effort with Louisiana are the major source of material for restoration of barrier islands located in the southwestern and central Louisiana coastal area.

---

### *Hurricane Sandy Supplemental Funding*

BOEM has played an important role in Hurricane Sandy recovery and resiliency efforts authorizing identification and use of sand resources offshore the Atlantic Coast for beach and habitat restoration projects. The depletion of sand deposits in state waters and the increasing frequency and intensity of coastal storms continues to elevate the demand for OCS sand and gravel resources along portions of the Gulf of Mexico and all along the Atlantic Coast. The demand for marine minerals has increased dramatically due to the coastal devastation along the Mid-Atlantic resulting from Hurricane Sandy.

To date, BOEM has received $13.6 million in supplemental funding for immediate needs related to Hurricane Sandy response, recovery and mitigation. These funds are allowing BOEM to support resource identification and delineation, to analyze potential environmental impacts, and to effectively manage OCS resources in response to Hurricane Sandy. All funding from Sandy Supplemental Appropriations will ultimately allow BOEM to provide OCS material to local, state and Federal agencies for nourishment, restoration and protection of parks, refuges, and other local, state, and Federal assets. The requests for additional information related to OCS sand resources has revealed a vulnerability or lack of knowledge regarding OCS sand resource availability necessary for shore protection. Through interaction with state agencies since Hurricane Sandy, it has become clear that identifying sand resources for nourishment projects is an elevated priority for many states.

Using the funds received thus far, BOEM is currently negotiating cooperative agreements with thirteen east coast states to fund various research efforts related to OCS data, resources and coastal resiliency; awards for all thirteen states are anticipated in 2014. Two million dollars has been awarded to the University of Florida ($1.5 million) and the Naval Undersea Warfare Center ($500,000) to conduct broad-scale environmental and ecosystem impact monitoring offshore Brevard County, FL. In addition to the funding received for response, recovery and mitigation, BOEM has responded to seven requests for the use of OCS sand and gravel for coastal restoration efforts along the entire eastern seaboard. Three agreements have been negotiated for Wallops Island, VA, Sandbridge Beach, VA, and Brevard County, FL, conveying approximately 2.75 million cubic yards of OCS sand. BOEM is currently working on five additional projects in response to Hurricane Sandy including Long Beach Island, NJ, Manasquan, NJ, Little Egg Harbor, NJ and Folly Beach, SC.

BOEM has closely coordinated with project partners and stakeholders including the U.S. Geological Survey, the U.S. Army Corps of Engineers, state governments, state geological surveys , local end-users, researchers, and industry to ensure efforts being taken for both research and construction projects are leveraged in an efficient and streamlined fashion.

Sand resource identification and delineation is critically important because identifying marine mineral resources and determining the sand deposit characteristics (sufficient quantity, appropriate grain size, environmental conditions or proximity to the placement site) enables the responsible management of these resources. Maintaining and expanding the inventory of OCS sand resources is critical to the Nation's coastal restoration and resiliency efforts. As the demand for these resources evolves, BOEM will seek to acquire new information about the availability and location of marine mineral resources on the OCS, as well as information on the environmental impacts associated with the removal of OCS sand.

> **Outlook on Conventional Energy**

In FY 2015, BOEM will continue to effectively and responsibly manage offshore energy and mineral resources. The management of these resources includes allowing for access to those resources, safeguarding a fair return to taxpayers, and applying the necessary environmental protection. Access to offshore energy and mineral resources will continue to be a high priority within BOEM, particularly the targeted efforts to develop the 2017-2022 Five Year Plan, the execution of scheduled oil and gas lease sales, and addressing the increasing need for OCS sand and gravel for the purposes of coastal restoration. Financial responsibilities, reduction of risks and economic evaluation and analysis of offshore natural resources will continue to be used to ensure the public receives a fair return for OCS energy resources. In addition, BOEM will continue to ensure the appropriate environmental protection measures are included in offshore activities including leasing of oil and gas and marine minerals. Looking forward, BOEM's Conventional Energy activities will continue to meet the high standards set forth by the Administration, Congress and the public through successful planning, execution and protection of the Nation's offshore resources in response to the Nation's energy needs.

# FY 2015 PERFORMANCE BUDGET
## Bureau of Ocean Energy Management
### *Environmental Programs*

### Table 15: Environmental Programs Budget Summary

|  |  | 2013 Actual | 2014 Enacted | Fixed Costs (+/-) | Program Changes (+/-) | 2015 Request | Change from 2014 (+/-) |
|---|---|---|---|---|---|---|---|
| **Environmental Programs** | ($000) | 60,578 | 63,218 | +200 | +2,294 | 65,712 | +2,494 |
|  | FTE | 148 | 150 |  |  | 150 | - |

## SUMMARY OF PROGRAM CHANGES

| Program Changes from 2014 Enacted | Amount ($000) | FTE |
|---|---|---|
| PEIS for 2017-2022 Five Year Program | +2,500 |  |
| Programmatic Reduction | -206 | - |
| **Total Program Changes** | **+2,294** | - |

The FY 2015 President's budget request for BOEM's Environmental Programs is $65.7 million and 150 FTE, a net change of +$2.5 million over the 2014 enacted level. This change is comprised of an increase in fixed costs of $200,000 and a net programmatic increase of $2.3 million.

**Programmatic Environmental Impact Statement (EIS) for the 2017-2022 Five Year Program (+$2,500,000; 0 FTE).** A thorough and completed programmatic EIS is required for BOEM's next Five Year Program (2017-2022). Not only is it mandated by NEPA, but it is also required in order to fullfill the requirements of the OCS Lands Act and BOEM's mission. The development of the programmatic EIS involves scoping, development of alternatives, Federal and state agency coordination, public comment, comment analysis and response, as well as publication of the draft and final programmatic EIS.

**Programmatic Reduction (-$206,000; 0 FTE).** In order to support BOEM's highest priority needs in FY 2015, the Bureau is proposing to reduce programmatic funding for Environmental Programs and realize additional savings by further implementing administrative restrictions on travel, training, and the filling of lower priority positions, similar to the measures taken during FY 2013.

## PROGRAM OVERVIEW

BOEM, in coordination with the Bureau of Safety and Environmental Enforcement (BSEE), is responsible for assessing the impacts of and providing effective environmental safeguards for the exploration and development of energy and mineral resources on the Outer Continental Shelf (OCS). This includes oil and gas, renewable energy resources (e.g., wind, wave, and tidal energy), and non-energy minerals such as sand and gravel. BOEM is also responsible for managing and ensuring environmental protection for any OCS activities for "marine-related purposes" (e.g., alternate use program) using facilities currently or previously authorized under the Outer Continental Shelf Lands Act.

These responsibilities require BOEM to assess the environmental impacts of planned and proposed OCS development and to provide guidance to developers and other stakeholders concerning the place, time, and nature of activities to be authorized. BOEM addresses these requirements through the Environmental Programs Activity (formerly the Environmental Assessment and Studies activity). This Activity is intended to inform decision-makers and the public about potential environmental impacts of OCS energy and mineral resource development, how to prevent or mitigate those impacts, and how to monitor impacts and measures for environmental protection. This information supports and guides decision-making not just within BOEM, but also by BSEE and by other government authorities.

> BOEM's environmental work on the OCS is guided by key laws such as:
> National Environmental Policy Act (NEPA)
> Coastal Zone Management Act
> Endangered Species Act
> Magnuson-Stevens Fishery Conservation & Management Act
> Marine Mammal Protection Act
> Clean Air Act
> Clean Water Act
> National Historic Preservation Act
> Migratory Bird Treaty Act

The Program includes the environmental assessment and the environmental studies functions described below. The environmental staff incorporates diverse expertise including marine and coastal biology, chemical and physical oceanography, avian and marine mammal biology, acoustic science, geology, meteorology, risk modeling, sociology, archaeology, environmental policy, and management. BOEM's environmental functions are organized administratively into the Office of Environmental Programs in the Washington, DC, area, including the Environmental Studies and Environmental Assessment Divisions; the Office of Renewable Energy Programs, also in the DC area; and the three BOEM regions: the Gulf of Mexico, Alaska, and the Pacific. While BOEM's science is managed as a single account through the Environmental Programs budget activity, it is the aim and practice of BOEM environmental staff to work in teams, with leadership provided by those whose backgrounds and capabilities best address the issues at hand. Furthermore, the Environmental Program is committed to continuous staff improvement through training and feedback and to recruitment and retention of the best talent available. The Program is also committed to partnerships and to genuine, continuing interaction with all stakeholders, including Federal, state, and local governments; tribes and other organizations of native peoples; civil society; and business.

## ENVIRONMENTAL ASSESSMENTS

BOEM's environmental assessment function addresses environmental impacts and the environmental requirements defined by a range of Federal statutes. Its work is informed by the best available science, drawing from the Environmental Studies Program and other research. The actions reviewed include authorization of geological and geophysical (G&G) exploration activities; plans for leasing; lease sales and approvals; exploration plans; development and production plans; and development operations coordination documents. The activity also reviews more specific authorizations and permits, including facility decommissioning, which may be approved and enforced by BSEE but whose environmental assessment is supported by BOEM. The Bureau's environmental assessments not only take a hard look at environmental impacts and alternatives to proposed actions, but they also identify measures to mitigate impacts which can be translated into requirements for operators through regulatory vehicles such as permit stipulations and notices to lessees.

➢ **Statutory Mandates**

At the very core of BOEM's Environmental Program is its mission to carry out the direction set forth by numerous and diverse legislative statutes. Under the OCS Lands Act, BOEM considers impacts from OCS development on the marine, coastal, and human environments. The impacts include not only the area within the OCS where energy and minerals resources are produced, but also geographic areas well beyond that may be directly or indirectly impacted by OCS development. The marine environment extends landward to salt marshes and wetlands. These coastal environments include the terrestrial ecosystem from the shoreline inward to the boundaries of the coastal zone, while the human environment includes the physical, social, and economic components that determine the state, condition, and quality of living conditions, employment, and health of those affected.

The OCS Lands Act and the National Environmental Policy Act (NEPA) establish the overall framework for BOEM's studies, assessments, and standards for environmental protection in resource development on the OCS. Environmental standards established by the OCS Lands Act differ with activity but include various key responsibilities for which BOEM and BSEE are now responsible. Among these is the responsibility to ensure that geological and geophysical activities will not be unduly harmful to aquatic life; that exploration for and production of oil and gas will not cause serious harm to the environment which cannot be modified to avoid the harm; that renewable energy production will be carried out in a manner that provides for protection of the environment; and that all applicable laws be complied with.

In accordance with NEPA and implementing regulations of the Council on Environmental Quality (CEQ), BOEM and other Federal agencies prepare an environmental impact statement (EIS), which includes an evaluation of alternatives, before taking a major action that will significantly affect the quality of the human environment. NEPA is BOEM's principal vehicle for reviewing environmental impacts and engaging public participation in the process. Programmatic environmental impact statements may be prepared initially if a proposed action is broad in nature (e.g. approval of a Five Year Program) and then followed by more specific subsequent environmental reviews that are "tiered" to the programmatic statement. While NEPA is one of the principle statutes that guides BOEM's environmental activities, other Federal laws give protection to specific resources that may be impacted by OCS activities authorized by BOEM. Both the Endangered Species Act and the Marine Mammal Protection Act provide an important framework for ensuring the health and safety of coastal habitats and wildlife.

The Endangered Species Act requires that BOEM not take any action likely to jeopardize the continued existence of any species listed as endangered or threatened or to destroy or adversely modify critical habitat of listed species. If an action by BOEM may affect a listed species, the Bureau is required to consult with either the National Marine Fisheries Service (NMFS), for primarily marine species, or the U.S. Fish and Wildlife Service (FWS), for species whose lives are more closely tied to land. As is the case for NEPA assessments, an Endangered Species Act consultation may be specific or programmatic. If any of the agencies involved believe that a formal consultation is warranted under the Act, then BOEM will prepare a biological assessment to inform itself and other Federal partners about the presence of listed species and impacts of the action on them. NMFS or FWS then reply with a biological opinion, which gives an opinion on whether the action is likely to jeopardize a listed species or adversely modify its critical habitat. Carrying out the principles espoused by the Endangered Species Act requires the highest level of scientific depth and quality, clarity in assessment, and coordination with the NMFS and FWS.

The Marine Mammal Protection Act (MMPA) is similarly dependent on the best available science and assessments to accomplish its mission. Avoiding and mitigating the potential harm for acoustic surveys for oil and gas reservoirs is an area of key focus for BOEM. The MMPA requires BOEM and other agencies to avoid injuring marine mammals or disrupting their behavior if there is more than "negligible impact" on the species. Recent efforts have focused specifically on the effects of air guns in seismic acoustic exploration on cetacean behavior.

BOEM's environmental assessment function also addresses the complex requirements of other laws including the Coastal Zone Management Act, with state program consistency generally required; the Magnuson-Stevens Fishery Conservation and Management Act, which requires review and protection of "essential fish habitat"; and, the Clean Air Act, which nationwide is typically managed by the U.S. Environmental Protection Agency (EPA) at the Federal level but for which the OCS in parts of the Gulf of Mexico and offshore the Alaska North Slope is managed by BOEM and BSEE. Other laws addressed include the Clean Water Act, administered by EPA at the Federal level; the National Historic Preservation Act, with particular focus on identifying and protecting shipwrecks and submerged settlements on the OCS; and, the Migratory Bird Treaty Act, whose restrictions on taking migratory birds are implemented by the FWS.

Fulfilling these diverse and critically important statutory mandates for protecting the environment guides the work of BOEM's environmental program. BOEM's science and assessment has a well-developed structure and process, but the core, essential purpose of the program, to which BOEM closely hews, is straightforward: to fulfill the direction of Congress for protecting the Nation's environment as energy resources are developed.

## ➤ Coordination with BSEE

Coordination with BSEE requires an additional, relatively new, effort by BOEM's Environmental Assessment staff. Since May 21, 2010, when Secretarial Order 3299 allocated responsibilities of the former Minerals Management Service to BOEM, BSEE, and the Office of Natural Resources Revenue (ONRR), BOEM has been responsible for more general decisions concerning OCS activities, such as approval of leasing plans, lease sales, explorations plans, and development and production plans. Consistent with BOEM's decisions, BSEE has been responsible for more specific decisions including issuance of permits to drill and other specific authorizations, stipulations, and conditions for operators, as well as enforcement.

Both BOEM and BSEE must comply with the laws generally applicable to Federal agencies, including NEPA, the Endangered Species Act, and the Marine Mammal Protection Act. In order to ensure maximum efficiency, BOEM and BSEE coordinate to avoid redundant reviews. As such, where there is common interest and the efforts lie within BOEM's scope and mission, BOEM will undertake or supplement studies, environmental assessments, and consultations with a view to providing the information and guidance needed for decisions by both BOEM and BSEE. This new interagency relationship requires a new level of effort for coordination and procedural integration.

## ➤ Major Cross-Cutting and Regional Assessments

BOEM's environmental assessments include the development of programmatic environmental impact statements for the Bureau's Five Year Program, for renewable energy activities, for G&G activities in the Atlantic, and for G&G activities in the Gulf of Mexico. BOEM's growing role in marine planning is likely to increase the use of programmatic EISs and comprehensive planning. Marine planning identifies areas most suitable for various types or classes of activities in order to reduce conflicts among uses, reduce environmental impacts, facilitate compatible uses, and preserve critical ecosystem services to meet economic, environmental, security, and social objectives.

BOEM follows programmatic statements with individual EISs, environmental assessments, findings of no significant interest, or determinations that a categorical exclusion applies. In this phased process, BOEM prepares hundreds of additional site-specific NEPA documents annually for decisions on proposed oil and gas operations, including operators' plans for exploration and development, pipeline permit applications, geophysical survey and geological sampling permit applications, structure removal, and other related industry activities. In FY 2013, BOEM completed over 500 environmental assessments for such activities following lease issuance.

In FY 2015, BOEM is requesting specific funding to continue work on a programmatic EIS for the next Five Year Program (2017-2022). The OCS Lands Act requires a completed programmatic EIS in order to move forward with a new oil and gas leasing program; the funding will be used to provide the environmental groundwork that will support the next Five Year Program. The programmatic EIS provides a concise assessment that addresses key issues throughout program implementation and provides information pertaining to environmental issues and Program alternatives. Additionally, the programmatic EIS provides insight and consideration regarding frontier areas in a Five Year Program. The funding will support contractor preparation of the programmatic EIS and also contractor facilitation of scoping meetings, public hearings, and government to government meetings. BOEM plans to enhance the traditional programmatic EIS through use of a new format to improve the EIS's accessibility and use in decision-making. The Bureau plans to prepare a more focused analysis of potential environmental impacts using the new geospatial analytical approach that presents impacts and issues largely through illustrative maps. This will allow BOEM to succinctly and effectively frame the most important issues related to the program decisions. The programmatic EIS will allow BOEM to more meaningfully communicate and interact with decision makers and the public.

***Assessments in the Gulf of Mexico Region:*** In the Gulf of Mexico, BOEM plans to finalize three major NEPA documents in FY 2014: a draft programmatic EIS for Gulf of Mexico G&G activities, prepared jointly with BOEM staff in the Washington, DC, area and with NOAA, and two supplemental EIS's considering new studies following the *Deepwater Horizon* explosion and oil spill, including available data from the Natural Resource Damage Assessment and Restoration process. These new activities will follow completion of a programmatic EIS for Atlantic G&G activities in FY 2014 and a supplemental EIS for lease sales in the Gulf's Central and Western Planning Areas that was completed in FY 2013. In FY 2014, BOEM also expects to prepare NEPA documents for decisions on Gulf Central and Western Planning Area lease operations, including G&G permit applications, pipeline applications, exploration plans, development operations coordination documents (including deep- and ultra-deep water activity), and facility decommissioning. In FY 2013, BOEM prepared NEPA documents for 299 plans; 103 pipeline applications; 57 G&G permit applications; applications for 34 ancillary activities; and, applications for 270 structure removals. BOEM expects FY 2014 and FY 2015 numbers to be the same or slightly higher.

**Walrus surfacing in Alaska**

***Assessments in the Alaska Region:*** BOEM's 2012-2017 Five Year Program includes sales in the Cook Inlet, Beaufort Sea and Chukchi Sea Planning Areas. Although the first of these sales, Chukchi Lease Sale 237, is not scheduled until calendar year 2016, the Alaska Region is already working on components of the NEPA analyses that will be used to support decisions regarding the sales in these areas. Presuming industry interest will increase in the Alaska OCS, BOEM must work diligently to keep pace.

More generally, BOEM is working with other agencies and stakeholders to understand the impacts of OCS activities on the Arctic marine environment. The Bureau is currently a cooperating agency to NMFS's lead in preparing a programmatic EIS for Arctic G&G activities and exploratory drilling, and BOEM will conduct NEPA analyses in FY 2014 and 2015 to support decision-making on exploration plans and specific G&G permits. The Alaska Region is committed to close interaction with Alaskan natives and the integration of traditional knowledge into interpretive documents and decision-making. Further, the cold winter temperatures and presence of ice add challenges to OCS development.

***Assessments in the Pacific Region:*** BOEM's Pacific Region conducts environmental assessments for conventional and renewable energy activities. Here BOEM's conventional energy assessments focus on development and production from 23 existing OCS facilities, largely in support of BSEE. Support for BSEE includes NEPA documents, assisting in enforcement of mitigation measures, and review of the measures' effectiveness.

BOEM expects to finalize the NEPA document for the Carpinteria Offshore Field Redevelopment Project in FY 2015. The project involves the use of an existing Federal platform for oil production from state leases. BOEM and the California State Lands Commission are jointly developing an environmental impact report/environmental impact statement for the various approvals for this project. Final decisions by BOEM and the California State Lands Commission are expected in FY 2015.

BOEM will also continue working with agencies and other stakeholders to advance research and commercial renewable energy projects on the Oregon and Hawaii OCS. WindFloat Pacific has submitted a commercial wind lease request to BOEM for a project offshore Coos Bay, Oregon, and the Bureau plans to complete an

**Carpinteria platform offshore California**

environmental review of the project by the first quarter of FY 2016 before making a decision on lease issuance. BOEM has also received a research lease request for a grid-connected wave energy test facility on the OCS offshore Newport, Oregon. The lease requires a FERC license in addition to BOEM approval, and the Bureau plans to cooperate with FERC on the environmental review before making a leasing decision.

Two draft commercial wind lease requests have been submitted to BOEM for an OCS area offshore the island of Oahu, Hawaii. BOEM will conduct environmental assessments of the requests if the Department of Defense determines the proposed use of the area is compatible with national security and military operations. BOEM also anticipates receiving a request as early as FY 2014 to authorize placement of an interisland cable for transmitting electricity between the islands of Oahu and Maui in Hawaii. BOEM expects to complete an environmental review of the request in FY 2016.

> ## Renewable Energy Assessments

The number of renewable energy environmental analyses in 2014 and 2015 will depend on the level of developer interest, and the time required to collect information for site assessment and construction operations plans. BOEM finalized NEPA documents for five designated wind energy areas offshore Delaware, Maryland, Massachusetts, New Jersey, Rhode Island, and Virginia during FY 2012 and FY 2013. BOEM anticipates completing documents in FY 2014 and FY 2015 for additional wind energy areas offshore Massachusetts and North Carolina. BOEM may also issue several limited research leases and transmission authorizations those years.

## ENVIRONMENTAL STUDIES PROGRAM

The Environmental Studies Program now managed by BOEM was first established in 1973 by the OCS Lands Act, which directed the Secretary of the Interior to –

- To establish information needed for the assessment and management of impacts on the human, marine, and coastal environments of the OCS and potentially affected coastal areas.

- To predict impacts on marine organisms resulting from a variety of factors: chronic low level pollution or large spills associated with OCS production; discharge of drilling muds and cuttings, as well as pipeline emplacement; and onshore development.

- To monitor human, marine, and coastal environments to provide time-series and data trend information for identification of significant changes in the quality and productivity of these environments.

BOEM's studies address each of these OCS Lands Act mandates. The discoveries and information generated through the Environmental Studies Program inform decisions by BOEM and BSEE concerning implementation of the OCS Lands Act, NEPA, the Endangered Species Act, the Marine Mammal Protection Act, and other applicable laws discussed above. The decisions include actions on regulations, measures for impact mitigation, stipulations to leases, notices to lessees, permits, and enforcement.

BOEM works to integrate science needs from multiple disciplines with respect to OCS energy and mineral resources (see Figure 12, below). In addition, BOEM considers studies independently underway to design and implement effective research for decision-making. A major, continuing emphasis is to understand the release, transport, fate, and effects of oil and other materials that may be discharged or spilled in the marine environment. Research on spill response is also a priority, conducted in close cooperation with BSEE's oil spill program.

**Figure 12: Environmental Studies Program Funds by Discipline**

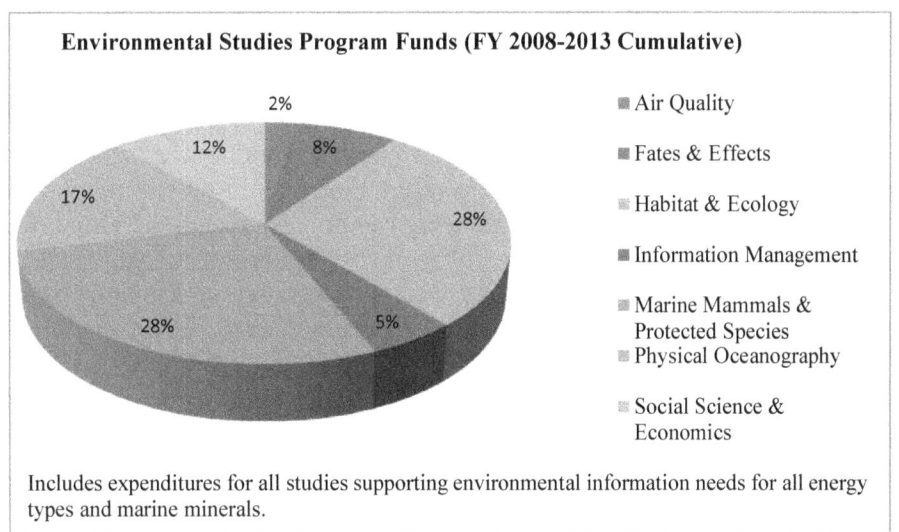

Includes expenditures for all studies supporting environmental information needs for all energy types and marine minerals.

Beginning in FY 2014, BOEM is developing a far-reaching, continuing collaboration with the National Research Council (NRC) of the National Academy of Sciences, with a view to establishing an NRC committee dedicated to the needs of BOEM. The committee's functions may include periodic comprehensive review of BOEM's programs; addressing questions of particular interest to the Bureau; participating in annual environmental study program reviews with the OCS Scientific Committee; providing peer review; facilitating stakeholder discussions of controversial issues; informally advising on recruitment; and providing facilities and support for meetings in Washington and at other locations where the National Academy has offices designed to facilitate scientific meetings. BOEM anticipates beginning support for this collaboration in FY 2014 and continuing support in FY 2015.

Because of its quality, scale, and duration, BOEM's Environmental Studies Program is a leading contributor to the growing body of scientific knowledge about the nation's marine and coastal environment. BOEM is committed to the highest level of scientific and scholarly integrity, as set forth by the Department of the Interior's Scientific and Scholarly Integrity Policy, by the Office of Science and Technology Policy, and by the President.

➢ **Research Partnerships**

Many BOEM studies are partnerships, including, for example, research addressing seismic noise impacts on marine mammals, environmental effects of sand and gravel extraction, real-time monitoring of environmental parameters, and long-term ecosystem monitoring in the Gulf of Mexico and in Alaska. Partnerships with Federal partners are typically through memoranda of understanding or agreement with individual agencies and through the National Oceanographic Partnership Program (NOPP), a collaborative community of Federal agencies working to improve knowledge of the ocean environment. For example, BOEM is currently supporting ship-based marine mammal and bird studies in cooperation with the FWS and NOAA. A new effort for FY 2014 involving NOPP is the "Marine Arctic Ecosystems Study: A Multi-Agency Partnership." This multi-agency project is intended to enhance arctic research coordination and improve regulatory decisions and NEPA analyses pertinent to lease sales in the Beaufort Sea, with the potential to include the Chukchi Sea.

Collaborations with the academic community are undertaken through BOEM-supported Coastal Marine Institutes located at the University of Alaska-Fairbanks and at Louisiana State University, as well as through several units within the Cooperative Ecosystem Studies Unit Network. These partnerships allow the contributing parties to leverage resources, extend the scope (both duration and area) of the research, and maximize the utility of results. Partners bring funds, equipment, facilities and personnel to support collaborative efforts. Many projects include opportunities to train students and contribute to the next generation of environmental leaders.

### BOEM's Award-Winning Studies

On January 16, 2014, Secretary Jewell announced the winners of the Department of the Interior's Partners in Conservation Award, including two partnerships from BOEM. The Partners in Conservation Awards recognize programs implemented through partnerships that represent excellence in conservation achievements; that further the Department's mission; that exemplify innovation and best practices for collaborative partnerships; and that build capacity for partnerships and conservation sustainability.

Two studies involving two BOEM partnerships recently won the DOI Partners in Conservation Award. One, titled "Developing Environmental Protocols and Monitoring to Support Ocean Renewable Energy and Stewardship," was developed in response to increased interest in offshore renewable energy. BOEM collaborated with the Department of Energy (Office of Energy Efficiency and Renewable Energy – Wind and Water Power Program) and NOAA's Office of Oceanic and Atmospheric Research, National Ocean Service, and NMFS using the NOPP framework. The partnership involved other Federal agencies, academic institutions, private companies and public stakeholders to conduct a suite of eight projects with a total value of $4.7 million. The partnership study topics broadly include baseline environmental information gathering, identification and evaluation of best management practices and protocols, evaluation of technologies for environmental assessment and monitoring, development of protocols and GIS tools to assist with facility siting, and the social and cultural implications of renewable energy development. All projects directly support sustainable management of energy by developing or providing baseline information for tools that assist managers in evaluating potential locations of offshore renewable energy facilities for appropriateness. These site-evaluation tools improve managers' ability to select appropriate offshore sites for leasing and development and to minimize conflicts with other uses and values.

The second award winner is "Exploration and Research of Mid-Atlantic Deepwater Hard Bottom Habitats and Shipwrecks with Emphasis on Canyons and Coral Communities." This collaboration is among diverse organizations, including three Federal agencies, 11 academic institutions, a state museum, and two private companies conducting research on deep-sea communities and historical shipwrecks off the mid-Atlantic coast. Utilizing cutting-edge technologies, including robotic underwater vehicles, benthic landers and instrumented moorings, results have included the discovery of abundant deep-water coral habitats and perhaps the largest methane seep community in the world. Knowledge of unique biological and cultural resources in deep water is necessary for offshore energy management decisions, and the science resulting from this study will be directly utilized by managers to strengthen the protection and conservation of these habitats from potential impacts related to energy development.

## ➢ The Studies Development Plan

BOEM's environmental studies include multiple layers of review to ensure that the best projects are selected. Each year, BOEM environmental staff solicit input from stakeholders and identify priority studies based on scientific merit, feasibility, relevance to decision-making (including timing), and cost. Potential studies are presented in an annual studies development plan that addresses a three year time horizon. The diagram in Figure 13 below shows the step-by-step process the Environmental Studies Program follows in putting together and carrying out the annual studies development plan.

**Figure 13: Environmental Studies Program Process Overview**

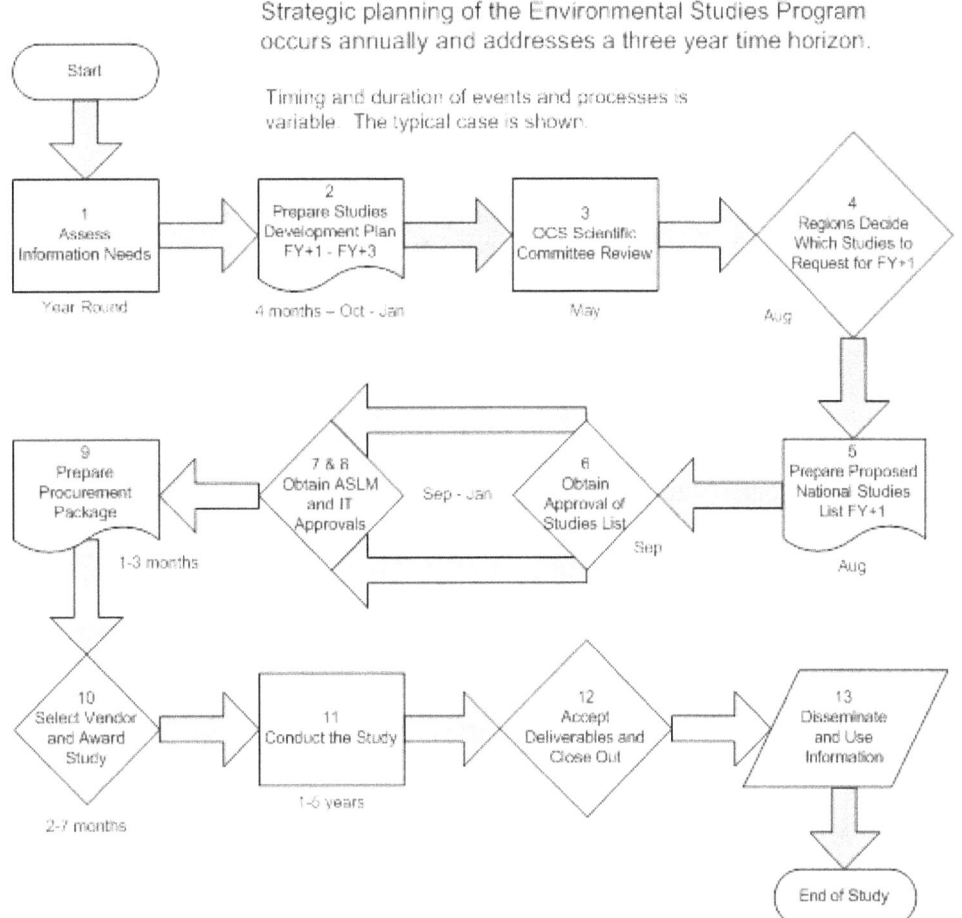

The study plan is peer reviewed internally through "subject matter expert" teams and others, and external review is provided by the OCS Scientific Committee, a Federal advisory committee whose 15 non-Federal members are appointed by the Secretary of the Interior. A representative from BOEM and a representative from NOAA serve as non-voting Federal members. The OCS Scientific Committee advises the Secretary, through the BOEM Director, on the feasibility, appropriateness, and scientific value of the program. Once proposed studies are critiqued by the OCS Scientific Committee, they are evaluated again before funding by program staff leadership, principally with reference to decision-making relevance, timing, and budget constraints. The study program is designed to be flexible and dynamic in order to accommodate changing circumstances or requirements. New information needs routinely arise outside the annual planning process, and, in response, proposed studies can be added, removed, or otherwise adjusted. This process of coordination ensures the acceptability of program products in the broader community and the applicability of the results to BOEM information needs, as well as those of BOEM's contributors and partners.

> **National Studies**

The studies development plan includes research relevant to knowledge and decision-making at all levels of government organization, and many studies are of global interest. These studies are currently grouped under the heading of "national studies" in the development plan and managed centrally by BOEM's Office of Environmental Programs, although BOEM's regional offices and Renewable Energy Program staff participate in and may lead projects. The fundamental distinction of national studies is that they are intended to address issues of recognized broad interest rather than of more specific interest to a region or program.

The national studies include a long-term partnership with the Smithsonian's National Museum of Natural History to preserve biological specimens from Federally-funded research, including sequenceable DNA, and to maintain and provide quality assurance for the databases associated with the specimens. In collaboration with NOAA, BOEM also supports MarineCadastre.gov – a website that allows visitors to view information concerning marine waters of the United States by geospatial units, including information on boundaries, infrastructure, human uses, energy potential, and other data sets. BOEM is specifically supporting work to enhance the website's public dissemination of environmental data sets, reports and other study products maintained by BOEM in its Environmental Studies Program Information System and in other systems.

Some specific examples of National-level studies planned for FY 2014 include:

- Developing BOEM's Access to Protected Species Occurrence Data for Impact Analyses and Rule-making

- Continued Archiving of Outer Continental Shelf Invertebrates by the Smithsonian Institution National Museum of Natural History

- Marine Arctic Ecosystems Study: A Multi-Agency Partnership

- Propagation Characteristics of High-Frequency Sounds Emitted During High-Resolution Geophysical Surveys

Information on the studies BOEM will undertake in FY 2014 is available through the BOEM website, and the list of planned FY 2015 studies will be available later this year. Studies planned in FY 2014 range from addressing the impacts of oil spills to evaluating impacts from new renewable energy development technologies to improving baseline characterizations and trend information. Special focus this year is given to work on marine mammals, birds, marine hydrokinetics, sea ice, air quality, and long-term and cumulative impacts, with an emphasis on partnerships to conduct studies.

BOEM's renewable energy program works with many agencies, universities and other stakeholders to identify critical data gaps in assessing the environmental impacts of renewable energy development in areas where it is likely to occur. In FY 2013, BOEM initiated three new studies to address Atlantic Coast science needs for renewable energy development, and six additional studies were launched in FY 2014. Current priorities are real-time observations of facility development, environmental and socioeconomic effects of port modifications, development impacts on marine mammals and birds, and effects of electromagnetic fields on biota. Several ongoing studies are expected to be completed in FY 2014 addressing bird abundance, hard bottom communities in canyons, air quality, cultural resources and the fates and effects of chemicals associated with wind turbines. The results of these studies will be used to inform BOEM decision-makers, environmental analysis, mitigation and monitoring protocols on environmental and cultural issues.

***Gulf of Mexico Region Studies:*** Long-term environmental monitoring is combined with experimental research to give Gulf of Mexico OCS decisions a firm scientific base. Studies in the Gulf of Mexico Region analyze and explore the ecology of every ocean province – from coastal marsh to ocean abyss – recognizing that oil and gas activities affect all habitats and that new technologies are facilitating activities in deeper waters. BOEM is especially challenged to provide the information and oversight needed for developing these new frontiers where biological and other environmental information currently is sparse and often outdated, and the Bureau emphasizes studies addressing deep waters of the Gulf offshore both the U.S. and Mexico.

**A remotely operated vehicle with sample jars**

One priority is additional deepwater current observations that can be used to validate the basin-wide ocean current model BOEM uses for the Gulf of Mexico. The *Deepwater Horizon* explosion and subsequent oil release have given impetus to revising baseline conditions and answering fundamental biogeochemical questions. For instance, a modeling effort is currently underway to hindcast the *Deepwater Horizon* oil spill plume in vertical and horizontal directions and to validate these results with available observations. More must be learned about the behavior of spilled oil and oil mixed with dispersants, particularly the interaction of dispersed oil with deepwater sediments. Post-*Deepwater Horizon*, the proliferation of damage assessments, recovery studies, and restoration projects provides a unique opportunity to develop a long-term comprehensive monitoring network that unifies existing monitoring programs and fills gaps in current monitoring. The challenge is to meet the needs of multiple ocean uses with a large-scale, integrated monitoring system that operates under common scientific goals to protect the environment, detect natural and anthropogenic change, and assess recovery.

*Alaska Region Studies:* BOEM's FY 2015 study efforts in the Alaska Region will focus on foundational research in the Beaufort and Chukchi Seas and new research in the Cook Inlet Planning Area. Strengthening collaborative research opportunities is a priority, including incorporation of traditional knowledge in research and interpretive materials. Other priorities are data synthesis; updating and improving oil spill risk analysis models; enhancing spill detection technologies and "nowcast" instrumentation; improving baseline monitoring of shore-zone habitats; improving ice forecast modeling; and generating a revised baseline for social indicators in North Slope communities. In FY 2015 BOEM plans to begin conducting broad seabed surveys in the Chukchi Sea that integrate bathymetry, archaeological resources, and ice gouge occurrence data. Future Cook Inlet research will focus on monitoring ecological processes and benthic invertebrate habitats.

*Pacific Region Studies:* In the Pacific Region, BOEM studies address the environmental impacts of oil and gas production, marine hydrokinetic wave energy conversion, and wind energy conversion. The area covered includes the OCS offshore California, Oregon, Washington, and Hawaii. Partners have a key role in Pacific Region studies: external stakeholders submitted eight proposals in FY 2013, including joint or individual proposals from the National Park Service, U.S. Geological Survey, Bureau of Land Management, NOAA, the State of California, and the State of Hawaii. All the proposals were reviewed through the studies program process, and funding priority was given for acquiring baseline information in areas where information is non-existent or limited, for studies to anticipate direct impacts at potential lease sites, and for monitoring offshore energy structures and devices after installation.

Biologists conducting rocky intertidal monitoring in CA

For conventional energy, the Pacific Region's priorities are better information for oil spill trajectory modeling and a synthesis of 30-years of research concerning how fish and invertebrate populations at oil and gas production platforms influence the marine ecology of the Pacific coast. Renewable energy study priorities include several issues for the OCS offshore Hawaii and Oregon. In Hawaii, BOEM's focus is locating submerged and shoreline cultural sites, determining seabird presence and ecology, performing a biogeographic assessment of marine species, and mapping human uses from the shore to the exclusive economic zone limit. In Oregon, priorities include observing the effect of power cables on species sensitive to electromagnetic fields, assessing benthic environments where facilities may be installed, and improving understanding of seabird oceanic flight behavior. In response to a request from the State of Oregon, BOEM worked with diverse experts to synthesize new research and existing information, to distill research into products that agencies and resource managers can use, and to identify and prioritize study gaps for technologies and potentially affected environmental systems. The results are published as *Oregon Marine Renewable Energy Environmental Science Conference Proceedings* and are available on BOEM's website.

## ➢ Outlook on Science and Environmental Programs

BOEM decisions and management of OCS oil and gas, marine minerals and renewable energy development will continue to be informed through the environmental assessments, studies and partnerships conducted under the Environmental Program. These efforts are vital to ensuring that the impacts of OCS activities on the environment are understood and the appropriate protective measures are put to use effectively. In direct support of BOEM activities, the Environmental Program will continue to focus the use of cross-cutting and regional environmental assessments for all OCS activities and regions including renewable energy, conventional energy and marine minerals. In particular, the funding requested in FY 2015 for the programmatic environmental impact statement will directly support the decision-making and development of the next Five Year Program. Through its environmental assessments and environmental studies, BOEM will continue to integrate science needs across programs and resources in order to effectively and timely inform decision makers. To these ends, BOEM will continue to utilize partnerships and will align and develop those partnerships to create an informed collaborative community with interest in OCS resources and a desire to protect the environment. Looking forward, BOEM's focus and dedication to using the most informative and up-to-date environmental information will continue, providing effective environmental safeguards for the development of OCS resources.

*This page intentionally left blank.*

# FY 2015 PERFORMANCE BUDGET
## Bureau of Ocean Energy Management
### *General Administration*

**Table 16: General Administration Budget Summary**

| | | 2013 Actual | 2014 Enacted | Fixed Costs (+/-) | Program Changes (+/-) | 2015 Budget Request | Change from 2014 (+/-) |
|---|---|---|---|---|---|---|---|
| **General Support Services** | ($000) | 12,149 | 14,320 | +728 | -46 | 15,002 | +682 |
| | FTE | 0 | 0 | | - | 0 | - |
| **Executive Direction** | ($000) | 15,223 | 16,256 | +116 | -53 | 16,319 | +63 |
| | FTE | 87 | 87 | | - | 87 | - |
| **TOTAL, General Administration** | ($000) | 27,372 | 30,576 | +844 | -99 | 31,321 | +745 |
| | FTE | 87 | 87 | | - | 87 | - |

The FY 2015 President's Budget for General Administration (General Support Services and Executive Direction combined) is $31.3 million and 87 FTE, a net increase of +$745,000. The net increase reflects the amount required to fund fixed costs, $844,000, offset by a program decrease of -$99,000.

The General Administration function provides the administrative, management, and policy support services crucial to carrying out BOEM's mission. The administrative arm of BOEM provides leadership and direction in overall management of the organization, planning and performance, budget, finance, human resources, information technology, and other services. Centralization of these administrative functions leverages resources and contributes to efficient and effective operations across the organization.

General Administration consists of two Activities:

- **Executive Direction**, which provides bureau-wide leadership both in headquarters and within the regions. It includes direction, management, coordination, budget, communications strategies, legislative and other external outreach, and regulatory and policy development.

- **General Support Services**, which ensures bureau-wide infrastructure support, such as office space, security, utilities, voice/data communications, and general administrative services.

# FY 2015 PERFORMANCE BUDGET
Bureau of Ocean Energy Management
*General Support Services*

## SUMMARY OF PROGRAM CHANGES

| Program Changes from 2014 Enacted | Amount ($000) | FTE |
|---|---|---|
| Programmatic Reduction | -46 | - |
| **Total Program Changes** | **-46** | **-** |

The FY 2015 President's budget request for BOEM's General Support Services is $15.0 million. This activity does not have any associated personnel costs. This reflects a net increase of $682,000 from the 2014 enacted level and is comprised of an increase for fixed costs of +$728,000 and a program decrease of -$46,000.

**Programmatic Reduction (-$46,000; 0 FTE).** In order to support high priority needs in FY 2015, the Bureau is proposing to reduce funding for General Support Services by minimizing administrative costs and imposing strict oversight of the administrative services provided through its reimbursable support agreement with BSEE.

## PROGRAM OVERVIEW

The General Support Services activity includes funding for shared activities and related support services for the entire Bureau. These expenses are administrative services provided to BOEM through a reimbursable service agreement with BSEE for finance, human resources, procurement, facilities, information management, and equal employment opportunity activities. Acquiring these critical services through BSEE minimizes the duplication of administrative functions in BOEM and BSEE and optimizes efficiency through the consolidation of resources into a single service provider.

The Department has strongly supported the expansion of business cross-servicing for more than 30 years. This latest effort between BOEM and BSEE is another step forward in this direction and will have the added benefit of implementing standardized practices that will further increase the productivity for highly skilled personnel in both bureaus. By utilizing the shared services model, BOEM and BSEE can continue to improve their best practices and maximize the use of administrative funds in the future.

Other related expenses funded under this activity include:

- Rental and security of office space

- Workers' compensation and unemployment compensation
- Voice and Data Communications
- The Department's Working Capital Fund
- Annual building maintenance contracts
- Mail services
- Printing costs

The two major program objectives are to provide safe and secure facilities that will contribute to the productivity and efficiency of the employees in achieving goals and objectives and to provide appropriate services in support of BOEM operating programs.

# FY 2015 PERFORMANCE BUDGET
## Bureau of Ocean Energy Management
### *Executive Direction*

## SUMMARY OF PROGRAM CHANGES

| Program Changes from 2014 Enacted | Amount ($000) | FTE |
|---|---|---|
| Programmatic Reduction | -53 | |
| **Total Program Changes** | **-53** | - |

The FY 2015 President's budget request for BOEM's Executive Direction is $16.3 million and 87 FTE. This reflects a net increase of +$63,000 from the 2014 enacted level. This change is comprised of an increase for fixed costs of $116,000 and a program decrease of -$53,000.

**Programmatic Reduction (-$53,000; 0 FTE).** In order to support BOEM's highest priority needs in FY 2015, the Bureau proposes to reduce programmatic funding for Executive Direction and realize additional savings by further implementing administrative restrictions on travel, training, and the filling of lower priority positions, similar to the measures taken during FY 2013.

## PROGRAM OVERVIEW

The Executive Direction Activity comprises the following: the Office of the Director; Office of Public Affairs; Office of Congressional Affairs; Office of Policy, Regulation and Analysis; Office of Budget and Program Coordination; and the Investigations and Review Unit.

### ➢ Office of the Director

The Office of the Director includes the BOEM Director and Deputy Director and their immediate staff, as well as the offices of the Regional Directors and their immediate staff. These components of the BOEM staff are responsible for providing policy guidance and overall leadership within the BOEM organization, as well as managing official documents within the Office of the Director.

### ➢ Office of Public Affairs

The Office of Public Affairs is responsible for BOEM's communication strategies and outreach. The Office of Public Affairs coordinates the implementation of an effective and inclusive outreach program to numerous target audiences, including state and local governments, the energy industry, related trade associations, the environmental community, tribes, energy consumer groups, and the public.

➢ **Office of Congressional Affairs**

The Office of Congressional Affairs serves as the primary point of contact with Congress and is responsible for the coordination of all communication and outreach with Congressional offices, as well as ensuring the effective exchange of information. The Office of Congressional Affairs serves as the liaison for BOEM on all Congressional and legislative matters that relate to BOEM's programs, including managing coordination with the Department of the Interior and other Federal executive agencies.

➢ **Office of Policy, Regulation and Analysis**

The Office of Policy, Regulation and Analysis serves as the principal office to lead and manage the bureau's national regulatory and policy programs and provides the Director with independent review and analysis of programmatic and management issues. Additionally, the Office of Policy, Regulation and Analysis leads, coordinates, and monitors many cross-program initiatives, assuring consistent BOEM-wide implementation that directly supports Congressional, Presidential, Departmental and Bureau directives, laws, mandates, and guidance. The office also fulfills the Director's responsibilities in several critical areas including regulatory management, activity-based costing, strategic and performance planning, policy, internal controls and program evaluation.

➢ **Office of Budget and Program Coordination**

The Office of Budget and Program Coordination is responsible for managing the budget planning process. The organization assesses current budgetary resources, provides recommendations for program and budget initiatives to senior BOEM executive staff, manages the personnel allocation system, and formulates and assists in the defense of BOEM's budget submissions to the Department, OMB, and Congress. In addition, the office is responsible for overseeing coordination with administrative service providers in the management of BOEM administrative activities and serves as the point of contact for any service-related questions.

➢ **Investigations and Review Unit**

During the transition, BOEMRE created the Investigations and Review Unit, which is composed of professionals with law enforcement backgrounds or technical expertise who promptly respond to allegations or evidence of misconduct and unethical behavior by Bureau employees. The Investigations and Review Unit also pursues allegations of misconduct against oil and gas companies involved in offshore energy projects when there is credible evidence that rules and regulations have been violated. The Unit is currently operating under BSEE and will work to identify BOEM and BSEE specific roles and responsibilities and assign staff to individual BOEM and BSEE units. Once the BOEM unit has been established, it will report directly to the Office of the Director.

*This page intentionally left blank.*

# Bureau of Ocean Energy Management
## FY 2015 Appropriations Language

The language provided below reflects changes from the Consolidated Appropriations Act, 2014, Public Law 113-76. As a general note, brackets indicate language to be deleted, and italics represent new language.

### OCEAN ENERGY MANAGEMENT

For expenses necessary for granting leases, easements, rights-of-way and agreements for use for oil and gas, other minerals, energy, and marine-related purposes on the Outer Continental Shelf and approving operations related thereto, as authorized by law; for environmental studies, as authorized by law; for implementing other laws and to the extent provided by Presidential or Secretarial delegation; and for matching grants or cooperative agreements, [$166,891,000]*$169,770,000*, of which [$69,000,000]*$72,422,000* is to remain available until September 30, [2015]*2016* and of which [$97,891,000]*$97,348,000* is to remain available until expended: *Provided*, That this total appropriation shall be reduced by amounts collected by the Secretary and credited to this appropriation from additions to receipts resulting from increases to lease rental rates in effect on August 5, 1993, and from cost recovery fees from activities conducted by the Bureau of Ocean Energy Management pursuant to the Outer Continental Shelf Lands Act, including studies, assessments, analysis, and miscellaneous administrative activities: *Provided further*, That the sum herein appropriated shall be reduced as such collections are received during the fiscal year, so as to result in a final fiscal year [2014]*2015* appropriation estimated at not more than [$69,000,000]*$72,422,000*: *Provided further*, That not to exceed $3,000 shall be available for reasonable expenses related to promoting volunteer beach and marine cleanup activities. *(Department of the Interior, Environment, and Related Agencies Appropriations Act, 2014.)*

### Proposed Language Changes:
BOEM does not propose any language changes in FY 2015.

The language provided below reflects General Provisions that are directly applicable to BOEM. For a complete, detailed discussion of the Department's proposed General Provisions, please refer to the General Provision chapter of the Office of the Secretary FY 2015 budget justification.

## GENERAL PROVISIONS, DEPARTMENT OF THE INTERIOR

### BUREAU OF OCEAN ENERGY MANAGEMENT, REGULATION AND ENFORCEMENT REORGANIZATION

SEC. 109. The Secretary of the Interior, in order to implement a reorganization of the Bureau of Ocean Energy Management, Regulation and Enforcement, may transfer funds among and between the successor offices and bureaus affected by the reorganization only in conformance with the reprogramming guidelines described in the report accompanying this Act.

**Proposed Language Changes:**
No language change to the General Provision is proposed in FY 2015.

# Bureau of Ocean Energy Management
## Proposals for Mandatory Accounts and Offsetting Collections

For a complete, detailed discussion of the Department's proposed General Provisions, please refer to the General Provision section of the Office of the Secretary FY 2015 budget justification.

**Federal Oil and Gas Reforms** – The 2015 Budget includes a package of legislative reforms to bolster and backstop administrative actions being taken to reform the management of Interior's onshore and offshore oil and gas programs, with a key focus on improving the return to taxpayers from the sale of these Federal resources and on improving transparency and oversight. Proposed statutory and administrative changes fall into three general categories: advancing royalty reforms, encouraging diligent development of oil and gas leases, and improving revenue collection processes.

Royalty reforms include evaluating minimum royalty rates for oil, gas, and similar products, adjusting the onshore royalty rate, analyzing a price-based tiered royalty rate, and repealing legislatively mandated royalty relief. Diligent development requirements include shorter primary lease terms, stricter enforcement of lease terms, and monetary incentives to get leases into production through a new per-acre fee on nonproducing leases. Revenue collection improvements include simplification of the royalty valuation process, elimination of interest accruals on company overpayments of royalties, and a permanent repeal of Interior's authority to accept in-kind royalty payments. Collectively, these reforms will generate roughly $2.5 billion in revenue to the Treasury over ten years, of which nearly $1.7 billion will result from statutory changes. Many states will also benefit from higher Federal revenue sharing payments as a result of these reforms.

The oil and gas reform package also includes a proposal to amend Section 365 of the Energy Policy Act of 2005 to extend the Act's permit processing pilot office authority beyond 2015 and remove the current limitation of the authority to only those pilot offices explicitly identified in the Energy Policy Act. This change will provide the Bureau of Land Management with greater flexibility in locating these offices where they can be most effective as industry permitting demands change over time. The pilot office authority allows BLM to fund personnel from other agencies that are assigned to these pilot offices. This authority has improved BLM's efficiency in processing Applications for Permits to Drill and other use authorizations. The 2015 legislative proposal does not extend the Permit Processing Improvement Fund that was also established by Section 365. This permanent funding source is scheduled to expire at the end of 2015.

*This page intentionally left blank.*

# Bureau of Ocean Energy Management
## Bureau Authorizing Statutes

### Outer Continental Shelf (OCS) Lands Program

| | |
|---|---|
| 43 U.S.C. 1331, et seq. | The Outer Continental Shelf (OCS) Lands Act of 1953, as amended, extended the jurisdiction of the United States to the OCS and provided for granting of leases to develop offshore energy and minerals. |
| P.L. 109-432 | The Gulf of Mexico Energy Security Act of 2006 required leasing certain areas in the Central and Eastern Gulf of Mexico Planning Areas within one year of enactment (December 20, 2006); and established a moratoria on leasing in remaining areas in the eastern planning area and a portion of the central planning area until 2022. |
| P.L. 109-58 | The Energy Policy Act of 2005 amended the OCS Lands Act to authorize the Department of the Interior to issue leases, easements and rights-of-way to develop renewable energy on the OCS and for certain other energy- and marine-related purposes using OCS facilities. |
| P.L. 133-67 | The Bipartisan Budget Act of 2013 amended OCSLA by authorizing the Secretary to take actions necessary to implement the U.S.-Mexico Transboundary Agreement with specific authority to carry out the agreement's provisions governing unitization, confidential information, inspections and dispute resolution. |
| 43 U.S.C. 4321, 4331-4335, 4341-4347 | The National Environmental Policy Act of 1969 required that federal agencies consider in their decisions the environmental effects of proposed activities and that Agencies prepare environmental impact statements for Federal actions having a significant effect on the environment. |
| 16 U.S.C. 1451, et seq. | The Coastal Zone Management Act of 1972, as amended, established goals for ensuring that Federal and industry activity in the coastal zone be consistent with coastal zone plans set by the States. |
| 16 U.S.C. 1531-1543 | The Endangered Species Act of 1973 established procedures to ensure interagency cooperation and consultations to protect endangered and threatened species. |

| | |
|---|---|
| 42 U.S.C. 7401, <u>et</u> <u>seq.</u> | The <u>Clean Air Act</u>, as amended, was applied to all areas of the OCS except the central and western Gulf of Mexico and the State of Alaska (as amended by P.L. 112-42). OCS activities in those non-excepted areas will require pollutant emission permits administered by the EPA or the States. |
| P. L. 112-42, Section 432 | The <u>Consolidated Appropriations Act of 2012</u> amended the Clean Air Act by transferring air quality jurisdiction from the EPA to the Department of the Interior for OCS activities in the Beaufort Sea and Chukchi Sea Planning Areas of the Arctic Outer Continental Shelf. |
| 16 U.S.C. 470-470W6 | The <u>National Historic Preservation Act</u> established procedures to ensure protection of significant archaeological resources. |
| 30 U.S.C. 1601 | The <u>Policy, Research and Development Act of 1970</u> set forth the continuing policy <u>et</u> <u>seq.</u> of the Federal Government to foster and encourage private enterprise in the orderly and economic development of domestic mineral resources and reserves. |
| 33 U.S.C. 2701, <u>et</u> <u>seq.</u> | The Oil Pollution Act of 1990, as amended, requires the responsible party for an offshore facility to maintain evidence of financial responsibility. It also provides for DOI to make inflation adjustments every three years to the $75 million limit on a responsible party's liability for damages for an unlawful oil discharge from an offshore facility. |
| 43 U.S.C. 1301 | The <u>Marine Protection, Research, and Sanctuaries Act of 1972</u> provided that the Secretary of Commerce must consult with the Secretary of the Interior prior to designating marine sanctuaries. BOEM provides information and comments regarding the mineral resource potential in areas being considered for designation as marine sanctuaries. |
| 16 U.S.C. 1361-1362, 1371-1384, 1401-1407 | The <u>Marine Mammal Protection Act of 1972</u> provides for the protection and welfare of marine mammals. |
| P.L. 104-58 | The <u>Deepwater Royalty Relief Act</u> provides royalty rate relief for certain offshore drilling leases in deepwater areas of the Gulf of Mexico. |

## General Administration

| | |
|---|---|
| 31 U.S.C. 65 | Budget and Accounting Procedures Act of 1950 |
| 31 U.S.C. 3901-3906 | Prompt Payment Act of 1982 |
| 31 U.S.C. 3512 | Federal Managers Financial Integrity Act of 1982 |
| 5 U.S.C. 552 | Freedom of Information Act of 1966, as amended |
| 31 U.S.C. 7501-7507 | Single Audit Act of 1984 |
| 41 U.S.C. 35045 | Walsh Healy Public Contracts Act of 1936 |
| 41 U.S.C. 351-357 | Service Contract Act of 1965 |
| 41 U.S.C. 601-613 | Contract Disputes Act of 1978 |
| 44 U.S.C. 35 | Paperwork Reduction Act of 1980 |
| 44 U.S.C. 2101 | Federal Records Act 1950 |
| 40 U.S.C. 4868 | Federal Acquisition Regulation of 1984 |
| 31 U.S.C. 3501 | Privacy Act of 1974 |
| 31 U.S.C. 3501 | Accounting and Collection |
| 31 U.S.C. 3711, 3716-19 | Claims |
| 31 U.S.C. 1501-1557 | Appropriation Accounting |
| 5 U.S.C. 1104 et seq. | Delegation of Personnel Management Authority |
| 31 U.S.C. 665-665(a) | Anti-Deficiency Act of 1905, as amended |
| 41 U.S.C. 252 | Competition in Contracting Act of 1984 |
| 18 U.S.C. 1001 | False Claims Act of 1982 |
| 18 U.S.C. 287 | False Statements Act of 1962 |
| 41 U.S.C. 501-509 | Federal Grant and Cooperative Agreement Act of 1977 |
| 41 U.S.C. 253 | Federal Property and Administrative Services Act of 1949 |

| | |
|---|---|
| 41 U.S.C. 401 | Office of Federal Procurement Policy Act of 1974, as amended |
| 15 U.S.C. 631 | Small Business Act of 1953, as amended |
| 15 U.S.C. 637 | Small Business Act Amendments of 1978 |
| 10 U.S.C. 137 | Small Business and Federal Competition Enhancement Act of 1984 |
| 15 U.S.C. 638 | Small Business Innovation Research Program of 1983 |
| 10 U.S.C. 2306(f) | Truth in Negotiations Act of 1962 Authorization |
| Secretarial Order No. 3299, Amendment No. 1 | Establishment of the Bureau of Ocean Energy Management (BOEM), the Bureau of Safety and Environmental Enforcement (BSEE), and the Office of Natural Resources Revenue (ONRR) in accordance with the authority provided by Section 2 of the Reorganization Plan No. 3 of 1950 (64 Stat. 1262). |
| Secretarial Order No. 3304 | Establishment of the Investigations and Review Unit (IRU) within the Bureau of Ocean Energy Management, Regulation and Enforcement in accordance with the authority provided by Section 2 of the Reorganization Plan No. 3 of 1950 (64 Stat. 1262), as amended. |
| Proclamation 5030 | Establishment of an Exclusive Economic Zone by the United States will advance the development of ocean resources and promote the protection of the marine environment, while not affecting other lawful uses of the zone, including the freedoms of navigation and overflight, by other States; 48 FR 10605, 3 CFR, 1983 Comp., p. 22 |

**Oil Spill Research**

| | |
|---|---|
| 33 U.S.C. 2701, et seq. | Title VII of the Oil Pollution Act of 1990 authorizes the use of the Oil Spill Liability Trust fund, established by Section 9505 of the Internal Revenue Code of 1986, for oil spill research. |
| 33 U.S.C. 2701, et seq. | Title I, Section 1016, of the Oil Pollution Act of 1990 requires a certification process which ensures that each responsible company, with respect to an offshore facility, has established, and maintains, evidence of financial |

responsibility in the amount of at least $150,000,000 to meet potential pollution liability.

43 U.S.C. 1331, et seq.

Section 21(b) of the Outer Continental Shelf Lands Act, as amended, requires the use of the best available and safety technologies (BAST) and assurance that the use of up-to-date technology is incorporated into the regulatory process.

Executive Order 12777

Signed October 18, 1991, assigned the responsibility to ensure oil spill financial responsibility for OCS facilities to the Secretary of the Interior (Bureau of Ocean Energy Management, Regulation and Enforcement).

*This page intentionally left blank.*

# Bureau of Ocean Energy Management
## Section 404 Compliance

Section 404 of Public Law 113-76, the Consolidated Appropriations Act, 2014, states:

*DISCLOSURE OF ADMINISTRATIVE EXPENSES*
*The amount and basis of estimated overhead charges, deductions, reserves or holdbacks, including working capital fund and cost pool charges, from programs, projects, activities and subactivities to support government-wide, departmental, agency, or bureau administrative functions or headquarters, regional, or central operations shall be presented in annual budget justifications and subject to approval by the Committees on Appropriations of the House of Representatives and the Senate. Changes to such estimates shall be presented to the Committees on Appropriations for approval.*

To improve efficiency, BOEM uses a shared services approach to meet its administrative needs. BOEM implements this approach through a reimbursable services agreement with BSEE, disclosed as internal administrative costs in the table below. Under this arrangement, BSEE provides a full suite of administrative services including acquisition management, equal employment opportunity, finance, human resources, information technology management, management support, personnel security, and support services. Maintaining these critical administrative functions within the Department provides the following benefits:

- Minimizing duplication of administrative entities across multiple organizations and optimizing efficiency.

- Providing a centralized administrative function that can, over time, allow the Department to pursue additional efficiencies.

The Department has strongly supported the expansion of business cross-servicing for more than 30 years. This latest effort between BOEM and BSEE is another step forward in this direction and will have the added benefit of implementing standardized practices that will further increase the productivity for highly skilled resources in both bureaus. By utilizing the shared services model, BOEM and BSEE can continue to improve their best practices and maximize the use of administrative funds in the future.

The BSEE regularly evaluates these support arrangements jointly with each customer agency. BSEE's costs to provide these services are also carefully managed and jointly approved by the respective agencies. Changes between cost allocations to BSEE and the customer agency may change to reflect actual agreements signed annually, and these changes would not be presented as a reprogramming.

The following table displays these costs as applied to the FY 2015 Budget.

| **Bureau of Ocean Energy Management** Overhead Charges, Deductions, Reserves, or Holdbacks *(dollars in thousands)* | |
|---|---|
| | **FY 2015** |
| **External Bureau Assessments** | |
| Executive Direction | |
| ASLM Support | 180 |
| IT Transformation | 74 |
| General Support Services | |
| Working Capital Fund Centralized Billing | 2,587 |
| Working Capital Fund Direct Billing | 793 |
| Zantas | 35 |
| NARA | 65 |
| Subtotal, External Assessments | $ 3,734 |
| | |
| **Internal Bureau Assessments** | |
| Renewable Energy | 1,475 |
| Conventional Energy | 6,616 |
| Environmental Programs | 5,290 |
| Executive Direction | 2,000 |
| General Support Services | 10,258 |
| Subtotal, Internal Assessments | $ 25,639 |
| | |
| **Total Assessments of Bureau Programs** | **$ 29,373** |

# Bureau of Ocean Energy Management
## Employee Count by Grade
### (Total Employment)

|  | 2013 Actuals | 2014 Estimate | 2015 Estimate |
|---|---|---|---|
| Executive Level V ................................. | 0 | 0 | 0 |
| SES ...................................................... | 5 | 6 | 6 |
| **Subtotal ...............................** | **5** | **6** | **6** |
| SL - 00 ................................................. | 0 | 0 | 0 |
| ST - 00 ................................................. | 0 | 0 | 0 |
| **Subtotal ...............................** | **0** | **0** | **0** |
| GS/GM -15 ........................................... | 36 | 36 | 36 |
| GS/GM -14 ........................................... | 114 | 116 | 117 |
| GS/GM -13 ........................................... | 167 | 170 | 171 |
| GS -12 .................................................. | 91 | 93 | 93 |
| GS -11 .................................................. | 43 | 44 | 44 |
| GS -10 .................................................. | 3 | 3 | 3 |
| GS - 9 ................................................... | 28 | 32 | 33 |
| GS - 8 ................................................... | 10 | 10 | 10 |
| GS - 7 ................................................... | 19 | 20 | 21 |
| GS - 6 ................................................... | 4 | 4 | 4 |
| GS - 5 ................................................... | 12 | 11 | 12 |
| GS - 4 ................................................... | 6 | 3 | 3 |
| GS - 3 ................................................... | 3 | 3 | 3 |
| GS - 2 ................................................... | 0 | 0 | 0 |
| GS - 1 ................................................... | 0 | 0 | 0 |
| **Subtotal ...............................** | **536** | **545** | **550** |
| Other Pay Schedule Systems ..................... | 0 | 0 | 0 |
| **Total employment (actuals & estimates) ...** | **541** | **551** | **556** |

Notes on this table:

- All grades presented in this table include career, career-conditional, temporary, and political employees.

- GS refers to employees covered by the General Schedule classification and pay system established under the Classification Act of 1949, as amended. (5 U.S.C. chapter 53, subchapter III, and 5 CFR part 531)

- GM refers to employees covered by the General Schedule classification and pay system who are covered by the Performance Management and Recognition System (PMRS) termination provisions of Public Law 103-89 (former PMRS employees).

www.ingramcontent.com/pod-product-compliance
Lightning Source LLC
Chambersburg PA
CBHW081110290526
45795CB00006B/2065